Teens and Alcohol

by Michael V. Uschan

LUCENT BOOKS
A part of Gale, Cengage Learning

Detroit • New York • San Francisco • New Haven, Conn • Waterville, Maine • London

LIBRARY OF CONGRESS CATALOGING-IN-PUBLICATION DATA

Uschan, Michael V., 1948-
  Teens and alcohol / by Michael V. Uschan.
    p. cm. -- (Hot topics)
  Includes bibliographical references and index.
  ISBN 978-1-4205-0749-2 (hardcover)
  1. Youth--Alcohol use. 2. Alcoholism--Prevention. 3. Drunk driving--Prevention. I. Title.
  HV5135.U83 2012
  362.2920835--dc23
                                        2011046548

Lucent Books
27500 Drake Rd.
Farmington Hills, MI 48331

ISBN-13: 978-1-4205-0749-2
ISBN-10: 1-4205-0749-4

Dedication

I dedicate this book to the members of Alcoholics Anonymous who shared their experiences as teenage drinkers with me to educate today's teens about the dangers of underage drinking Hawk, Gary, Greg, Jack, Jeff, Judy, and Mike.

Printed in the United States of America
2 3 4 5 6 7 16 15 14 13 12

CONTENTS

FOREWORD

Young people today are bombarded with information. Aside from traditional sources such as newspapers, television, and the radio, they are inundated with a nearly continuous stream of data from electronic media. They send and receive e-mails and instant messages, read and write online "blogs," participate in chat rooms and forums, and surf the Web for hours. This trend is likely to continue. As Patricia Senn Breivik, the former dean of university libraries at Wayne State University in Detroit, has stated, "Information overload will only increase in the future. By 2020, for example, the available body of information is expected to double every 73 days! How will these students find the information they need in this coming tidal wave of information?"

Ironically, this overabundance of information can actually impede efforts to understand complex issues. Whether the topic is abortion, the death penalty, gay rights, or obesity, the deluge of fact and opinion that floods the print and electronic media is overwhelming. The news media report the results of polls and studies that contradict one another. Cable news shows, talk radio programs, and newspaper editorials promote narrow viewpoints and omit facts that challenge their own political biases. The World Wide Web is an electronic minefield where legitimate scholars compete with the postings of ordinary citizens who may or may not be well-informed or capable of reasoned argument. At times, strongly worded testimonials and opinion pieces both in print and electronic media are presented as factual accounts.

Conflicting quotes and statistics can confuse even the most diligent researchers. A good example of this is the question of whether or not the death penalty deters crime. For instance, one study found that murders decreased by nearly one-third when the death penalty was reinstated in New York in 1995. Death penalty supporters cite this finding to support their argument that the existence of the death penalty deters criminals from committing murder. However, another study found that states without the death penalty have murder rates below the national average. This study is cited by opponents of capital punishment, who reject the claim that the death penalty deters murder. Students need context and clear, informed discussion if they are to think critically and make informed decisions.

The Hot Topics series is designed to help young people wade through the glut of fact, opinion, and rhetoric so that they can think critically about controversial issues. Only by reading and thinking critically will they be able to formulate a viewpoint that is not simply the parroted views of others. Each volume of the series focuses on one of today's most pressing social issues and provides a balanced overview of the topic. Carefully crafted narrative, fully documented primary and secondary source quotes, informative sidebars, and study questions all provide excellent starting points for research and discussion. Full-color photographs and charts enhance all volumes in the series. With its many useful features, the Hot Topics series is a valuable resource for young people struggling to understand the pressing issues of the modern era.

INTRODUCTION

Teens + Alcohol = Trouble

Shortly after 5:00 A.M. on June 17, 2011, Keaton Leon Hannah ran into the rear of another vehicle while driving his pickup truck on Oklahoma State Highway 66 in Verdigris, Oklahoma. It was only a minor accident, but Hannah was only eighteen and he had been drinking. Fearing that he would be arrested for drunk driving, Hannah turned his truck around and sped away from the scene of the crash. Driving the wrong way on the westbound lanes of the highway, Hannah smashed head-on into a sports utility vehicle with three people in it. Hannah suffered only minor injuries, but the crash killed twenty-one-year-old Eric Watkins and his eight-month-old son, Bryor.

Hannah was charged with two counts of first-degree manslaughter—charges that carry a penalty of life in prison—and one count of leaving the scene of an accident. Verdigris police chief Barry Lamb said the deadly crash had tragic consequences for both parties involved: "You've got the one family that has paid the ultimate price for another person's actions and then you've got this young man who's whole future is sacrificed on a silly decision."[1] The teenager's decision to drink killed two people and resulted in dire consequences for his future—he was charged with serious crimes and for the rest of his life would also have to live with feelings of guilt and remorse for the deaths of two people.

Fatal drunk driving accidents are the most highly publicized incidents involving teenagers who drink. But when teens drink, being arrested for killing someone in an auto accident is just one of the many bad things that can happen to them.

Teen Drinking Is Dangerous

In 2007 acting U.S. Surgeon General Kenneth P. Moritsugu issued a report on the scope of underage drinking and the dangers teens face when they drink. The surgeon general, the nation's top public health official, wrote:

> Underage alcohol consumption in the United States is a widespread and persistent public health and safety problem that creates serious personal, social, and economic consequences for adolescents, their families, communities, and the Nation as a whole. By age 15, approximately 50 percent of boys and girls have had a whole drink of alcohol; by age 21, approximately 90 percent have done so.[2]

The legal drinking age in all fifty states is twenty-one, which means that the millions of teenagers who drink are breaking the law. Because drinking is illegal for teens, police can arrest them just for possessing alcoholic beverages. School officials can also punish students for drinking even if it did not take place in school. For example, schools often ban athletes from participating in sports if they consume alcohol. Teenage drinkers can also expect to be disciplined by their parents.

Teenagers who drink however, face a much greater risk than being arrested or scolded by their parents. A 2006 study by the National Research Council and Institute of Medicine showed that approximately 5,000 young people under the age of 21 die each year as a result of drinking. These deaths include about 1,900 fatalities in motor vehicle crashes, 1,600 homicides, 300 suicides, and hundreds of deaths from causes such as falls, burns, or drowning. The most dangerous situation for teens is when they drive or are passengers in cars driven by teens who have been drinking. A 2009 National Highway Traffic Safety Administration study of traffic accidents involving teens noted that traffic accidents, many of which involved drinking, were the leading cause of death for U.S. teenagers: "Young drivers, ages 15- to 20-years old, are especially vulnerable to death and injury on our roadways—traffic crashes are the leading cause of death for teenagers in America. Mile for mile, teenagers are involved in three times as many fatal crashes as all other drivers."[3]

In the United States, underage consumption of alcohol is a widespread and persistent public health and safety issue that creates serious personal, social, and economic consequences for teens, their families, and communities.

The study showed that 35 percent of all teenage deaths in 2009 were due to motor vehicle accidents. That figure was more than twice the second- and third-leading causes of teenage deaths—homicide (16 percent) and suicide (12 percent)—and just slightly less than all other causes of teenage death combined (37 percent).

Teens risk their lives just by drinking alcohol. Their lack of experience with the powerful physical and psychological effects alcohol creates in people can lead them to drink more dangerously than adults. On March 13, 2011, Molly Ammon, a nineteen-year-old University of Florida freshman, died from alcohol poisoning after drinking heavily at a party in Madeira Beach, Florida. Her blood alcohol concentration (BAC) was 0.408 percent, nearly five times the legal limit considered proof of drunk driving. Excessive drinking is common for teenagers because they tend to drink as much as they can when they have access to alcohol. The Centers for Disease Control and Prevention (CDC) has reported that drinkers age twelve to twenty consume more than 90 percent of the alcohol they drink during such episodes of binge drinking. In the Ammon case what was supposed to be a good time turned deadly. Tampa mayor Pam Iorio, who knew Ammon, said, "It's such an awful tragedy that it's hard for everyone to even absorb it. Molly was a beautiful young woman, full of life. This is absolutely devastating."[4]

In 1992 Joseph A. Califano Jr., a former secretary of Health, Education, and Welfare, founded the National Center on Addiction and Substance Abuse. An expert on drug abuse, Califano has written and commented extensively on teenage use of alcohol and other drugs. Califano believes alcohol is more dangerous for teens than illegal drugs like marijuana or cocaine. He claims, "The media focuses on illegal drugs like heroin, but that's the tail. The dog is alcohol and the dog is really biting our kids."[5] Like many people, Califano believes alcohol causes more problems than other drugs for teens because it is easier to obtain and because they know they will be able to drink legally in just a few more years.

But when teens get their hands on alcohol, even good kids who rarely get into trouble can suffer terrible consequences. Keaton Leon Hannah is an example of that.

"A Good Kid"

Hannah's drunk driving crash that killed two people stunned his community. He lived in Claremore, Oklahoma, and was a youth minister at Destiny Life Church. Jeremy Donovan, youth pastor at the church, said he felt bad for both the Watkins family and Hannah, whom he said was a good young man: "There's a lot of kids here that knew Keaton. He was a good kid and made some [bad] choices."[6] It was the choice Hannah made to drink that led to the incident that ruined his life. When the *Tulsa World* newspaper ran a story about the crash on its website, many people posted their reactions. One comment harshly criticized Hannah:

> [Hannah] drank while not legal to drink (mistake one), he drove while intoxicated (mistake two), caused an accident (mistake three), left the scene of an accident (mistake four), drove the wrong way on a highway (mistake five), caused another accident (mistake six), killed TWO people (mistake seven and mistake eight). At ANY point he could have stopped and said enough . . . but he decided to KEEP breaking the law each step of the way . . . ALL THE WAY TO KILLING PEOPLE![7]

The results of Hannah's decision to drink were horrendous, both to friends and families of the victims and Hannah himself.

ALCOHOL: A SOCIALLY ACCEPTED DRUG

Teenagers in the United States use alcohol more often than any illegal drug. In 2010 the National Institute on Drug Abuse released statistics that showed 71 percent of teens had tried alcohol by the time they reached the twelfth grade even though they were not yet twenty-one, the legal drinking age in all fifty states. The institute also reported that 65.2 percent of teens had drunk an alcoholic beverage within the past year. Such widespread use of alcohol compared to 43.8 percent of teens who had experimented with marijuana by the twelfth grade, 9 percent who had tried inhalants, and 8.6 percent who had ingested hallucinogens. In their book about teenage drug use, Katherine Ketcham and Nicholas A. Pace explain that one reason so many teens try alcohol is that they mistakenly believe it is harmless compared to drugs like cocaine that are illegal for adults as well as teens. Ketcham and Pace write: "MYTH: Alcohol isn't really a drug—at least it's not as bad as LSD, cocaine, marijuana, amphetamines, or heroin. FACT: Alcohol is a toxic, potentially addictive drug that causes more damage to the individual and society than all illegal drugs combined—in fact, alcohol kills nearly seven times more young Americans than all illegal drugs combined."[8]

The dangers alcohol poses to everyone—adults as well as teenagers—include being killed in a drunk driving accident as either a driver or passenger and dying from alcohol poisoning if a person consumes too much during a binge drinking session. In addition, alcohol is often cited as a factor in suicides and homicides. It can also lead drinkers to engage in risky behavior that can harm or kill them, like car surfing, which involves riding on the hood of a car. Because their bodies and brains are not yet fully developed, however, teenage drinkers face several risks that adults do not. Alcohol can damage teenage brains because they are still changing and developing. And people who start drinking in their teens face a higher risk of becoming an alcoholic than those who wait to drink until they are older.

Many teens see nothing wrong with underage drinking, especially since alcohol use is such a part of American society.

Ignorance about the dangers of drinking makes it easy for teenagers to believe alcohol is a benign drug. However, teenagers also have trouble understanding the dangers of alcohol because of society's nearly universal acceptance of drinking, even heavy drinking on special occasions like birthday parties or weddings. This is especially true if their parents or other relatives drink. In *A Six-Pack and a Fake I.D.*, Susan and Daniel Cohen explain that the approval society gives to using alcohol makes it hard for teenagers to believe they are doing anything wrong when they drink, even though they are not old enough to do it legally:

> Alcohol is a drug that is woven into the very fabric of our society. Drinking is part of our history and heritage. It's not going to go away. Since drinking is legal, and what is more important quite acceptable to the vast majority, the social context in which drinking takes place is vastly different from that in which other drugs are used. And that is a vital difference between alcohol and other drugs.[9]

Society's acceptance of drinking is so strong that Gail Gleason Milgram, an expert on alcohol abuse, says, "Alcohol is the drug of choice for most Americans."[10] This positive attitude toward drinking is rooted in the historic use of alcohol, which extends back thousands of years.

Alcohol's Historic Roots

Ethyl alcohol is the chemical in alcoholic beverages like beer, wine, and whiskey that intoxicates people. Alcohol is produced by fermentation, a chemical reaction that occurs when yeast reacts with food that contains sugar, such as fruits, berries, and grains. Fermentation occurs naturally because yeast can be microscopic and float freely in the air. When ancient humans consumed accidentally fermented berries and became drunk, they must have been mystified as to why berries they normally ate for sustenance made them feel so strange.

No one knows when or how people first discovered how to make alcoholic beverages. The earliest evidence of alcoholic drinks is from jars found in China that date back to 7000 B.C., which means people have been consuming alcoholic beverages for nine thousand years. The Chinese jars had traces of an alcoholic beverage made by fermenting rice, honey, and fruit. The most widespread early alcoholic drink was beer. Clay tablets found in the ruins of ancient Babylon that are seven thousand years old are the earliest written record that prove people drank beer. Evidence also exists that Egyptians brewed beer thousands of years ago. They called the beverage *hek*. They made it by crumbling barley bread into jars, covering it with water, and allowing the yeast in the bread to ferment naturally.

Beer and wine produced through natural fermentation have low alcohol contents, about 5 to 8 percent for beer and 12 percent for wine. People living in virtually every part of the world have consumed such drinks for thousands of years. Brandy, whiskey, and other distilled beverages, which are called spirits, have a much shorter history. Distillation was discovered first in Arabia in the eighth century and then in Europe in the twelfth century. Distillation produces concentrated alcohol and allows beverages to have alcohol contents ranging from 20 percent to 60 percent, far higher than naturally fermented beer and wine. The higher alcohol content in spirits enables people to become drunk by drinking much smaller portions of them than beer or wine.

There were many reasons alcoholic beverages became a normal part of everyday life. Many people enjoy consuming alcohol because it can change their mood and usually make them feel happier. Centuries ago people also drank alcoholic beverages because so many sources of water and milk were contaminated that people risked getting diseases like cholera if they consumed them. For example, President Abraham Lincoln's mother died after drinking milk from a cow that had eaten a poisonous weed.

Alcoholic beverages were also an important food source for people with limited diets that were low in calories. This was especially true in Europe, where widespread poverty made it hard for people to buy enough food. In 1551 historian Johann Brettschneier described how average people depended greatly on beer for nourishment: "Some subsist more upon this drink than they do on food. People of both sexes and every age, the hale and

The making of alcohol has always been a part of human life. In this painting from an Egyptian tomb from the fifteenth century B.C. workers are shown brewing beer.

the infirm alike, require it."[11] Because alcohol has a sedative effect that can ease pain from injury, illness, and hard labor, employers gave alcohol to workers to help them work harder and longer. Sailors and soldiers, for example, received daily rations of rum.

In ancient times alcohol was also used for many medical purposes, such as dressing wounds and fighting fever. The medicinal qualities of wine were held in such high regard that the Talmud, the main religious text of Judaism, claims, "Wine taken in moderation induces appetites and is beneficial to health. Wine is the greatest of medicines."[12] And the Christian Bible's New Testament advises readers to "no longer drink water exclusively, but use a little wine for the sake of your stomach and your frequent ailments."[13] Wine even plays a central part in Christian worship—when people receive Communion, they usually take a sip of wine.

An Alcoholic Republic

When English colonists immigrated to the land that would become the United States, they brought such favorable attitudes about alcohol and drinking traditions with them. On May 14, 1607, the first British colonists arrived in North America and established Virginia, the first of thirteen colonies that would eventually break away from England and become the United States. Thirteen years later, on December 21, 1620, the Pilgrims landed off the coast of what would become Massachusetts. The importance of alcoholic beverages to the Pilgrims is evident; among the supplies the 102 passengers brought to the New World were 12 gallons (45L) of distilled spirits and 10,000 gallons (37,854L) of beer. Beer was considered vital because in seventeenth-century England the average person, even a child, drank about 3.2 quarts (3L) of beer per day. Children, however, drank beer whose alcohol content was lower than the beer adults drank.

Increase Mather, a prominent minister in Boston in the early 1700s, famously stated the positive attitude colonists had toward alcohol when he wrote that it was "the good creature of God [and was] to be received with thankfulness."[14] Alcohol even played an important role in the nation's founding. In *The Alcoholic Republic: An American Tradition*, W.J. Rorabaugh writes, "Patriots [colonists who opposed British rule] viewed public houses [taverns] as the nurseries of freedom" and even claimed they were "certainly seed beds of the Revolution, the places where British tyranny was condemned, militiamen organized, and independence plotted."[15] Conversations over mugs of beer and

Prominent Boston minister Increase Mather wrote about the positive attitude of American colonists toward alcohol in the early 1700s.

sips of whiskey helped spark the American Revolution, the war that resulted in the establishment of the United States in 1783 when colonists won their freedom by defeating the British.

FAVORED BEVERAGE

"The levels of [alcohol] consumption in colonial America have never been surpassed [by Americans in any other period of its history]; for eighteenth-century Americans alcohol was considered safer and healthier than water."—James B. Jacobs, author and professor of constitutional law and the courts at New York University

James B. Jacobs. *Drunk Driving: An American Dilemma.* Chicago: University of Chicago Press, 1989, p. 5.

Residents of the new nation drank even more after the war. By the 1830s the average American aged fifteen or older consumed 7 gallons (26.5L) of pure alcohol (100 percent alcohol) annually. That figure is more than twice the 2007 alcohol consumption rate of Americans fourteen or older, which was 2.31 gallons (8.74L). Per capita annual consumption in the 1830s included 9.5 gallons (35.96L) of spirits, 1 to 2 gallons of wine (3.79L to 7.57L), and 27 gallons (102.2L) of beer each year. Historian Thomas R. Pegram describes the young nation's lenient attitude toward drinking:

> Although community scorn and the power of law was brought to bear on drunkards, everyone was expected to consume alcoholic beverages as dietary staples, and over-indulgence was tolerated at weddings, funerals, militia musters, and on holidays. Women drank in the home; men drank more frequently and more copiously at home, in the fields or the shop, and at taverns and during public events such as elections; solicitous parents shared beer with children at meals, and encouraged boys to develop a taste for distilled spirits.[16]

The increasingly high drinking levels of many Americans during the eighteenth and nineteenth centuries led to public

Liquor for Soldiers

In the eighteenth and nineteenth centuries, employers often gave their workers alcoholic beverages during the workday because they believed the energy workers received from the calories in beer and alcohol would make them more productive. Farmers gave workers jugs of rum or brought beer to them while they were working in fields planting or harvesting crops. Even Roman Catholic nuns were given a ration of alcohol each day. Those receiving daily rations of alcohol also included soldiers and sailors. George Washington led colonists to victory during the Revolutionary War and afterward became the nation's first president. Historian Eric Burns claims Washington firmly believed alcohol made his soldiers better fighters:

> During the Revolutionary War, George Washington insisted on alcohol for his men, and once, when a shipment was delayed, he wrote an anguished letter to the president of the Continental Congress: "The benefits arising from the moderate use of strong Liquor," Washington stated, "have been experienced in all Armies and are not to be disputed."

Quoted in Eric Burns. *Spirits of America: A Social History of Alcohol*. Philadelphia: Temple University Press, 2004, p. 16.

drunkenness becoming common, incidents of violence, and other social problems. Such alcohol-related problems created a backlash against drinking and spurred attempts to limit and even ban its consumption.

An Experiment That Failed

Although most people in the eighteenth and nineteenth centuries drank alcoholic beverages at home as a source of food or because water was unsafe, many people began drinking in public houses, the British name for businesses serving alcohol. Many public houses—Americans were soon calling them taverns, saloons, and bars—became centers of criminal activity like gambling and prostitution. Even taverns free of such vices were criticized because their owners encouraged patrons to engage in heavy drinking. There were so many public houses in Philadelphia in 1744 that a grand jury studied the situation. The report claimed public houses were "little better than Nurseries of Vice and Debauchery, and tend to increase the Number of our Poor."[17] Most taverns in Philadelphia were located in a part of the city that became known as Hell Town because of the trouble drunken patrons caused.

In 1826 Presbyterian minister Lyman Beecher helped found the American Temperance Society in Boston. Beecher claimed drinking was dangerous because too many people could not stop once they began: "Much is said about the prudent use of spirits, but we might as well speak of the prudent use of the plague—of fire handed prudently round among [gun]powder—of poison taken prudently every day."[18] In its first five years, the society established 2,220 local chapters throughout the United States and attracted 170,000 members who pledged to quit drinking; within a decade the society had over 8,000 groups and more than 1.5 million members.

THE SALVATION OF SOCIETY

"The reign of tears is over. The slums will soon be a memory. We will turn our prisons into factories and turn jails into storehouses and corn-cribs. Men will walk upright now, women will smile and the children will laugh."—The Reverend Billy Sunday's prediction when Prohibition became law

Quoted in Eric Burns. *Spirits of America: A Social History of Alcohol.* Philadelphia: Temple University Press, 2004, p. 187.

In the second half of the nineteenth century, more militant groups like the Anti-Saloon League and the Woman's Christian Temperance Union staged public protests against drinking. The demonstrations often included attacks on saloons by ax-wielding protesters like Carry Nation, who smashed barrels of beer and whiskey. In 1846 Maine passed a law prohibiting the sale of alcohol. Few other states, however, did much to regulate alcohol. Concern about the problems drinking caused kept growing, and on June 29, 1919, the nation ratified the Eighteenth Amendment

Was Prohibition a Failure?

The Eighteenth Amendment banning the sale and consumption of alcoholic beverages went into effect on January 16, 1920, and lasted until December 5, 1933, when the Twenty-First Amendment repealed it. Prohibition drastically reduced alcohol consumption, but millions of Americans continued to drink despite the fact that it was illegal. Even though Prohibition ended because a majority of Americans demanded the right to drink, historian Robert Kelley claims Prohibition had some beneficial effects. He writes that notorious saloons in big cities that were homes to vice were closed during Prohibition and that after Prohibition, government officials regulated such businesses more closely. Kelley also says Prohibition changed the nation's drinking habits:

Drinking in America had been fundamentally changed by the Prohibition experiment. Cheap liquor would never be available again so readily as in the past. Drinking to excess in public, so common before Prohibition, had lost much of its macho appeal. [And a new] general ethic of moderation in drinking would mean that repeal, when it finally came in 1933, would see not a revival of the old, but entry into a new national relationship with alcohol.

Robert Kelley. *The Shaping of the American Past: 1865 to Present*. Englewood Cliffs, NJ: Prentice Hall, 1990, p. 576.

Revenue agents show off confiscated liquor from a raid on a Prohibition-era speakeasy. By the time Prohibition was repealed in 1933 Americans had developed a new relationship with alcohol.

to the Constitution. The amendment prohibited making or selling any beverage with more than 0.5 percent alcohol, a level so low that it would not make people drunk.

PROHIBITION WILL NOT SAVE US

"Prohibition only drives drunkenness behind doors and into dark places, and does not cure or even diminish it."—Mark Twain, who did not live to see Prohibition but firmly believed any attempt to stop people from drinking would fail

Quoted in Paul Sann. *The Lawless Decade: A Pictorial History of a Great American Transition: From the World War I Armistice and Prohibition to Repeal and the New Deal.* New York: Bonanza, 1957, p. 92.

Prohibition went into effect on January 16, 1920, but quickly proved to be a failure. Criminals like Chicago's Al Capone became millionaires by supplying beer and liquor to people who chose to break the law and drink anyway. The law was so openly ignored and generally hated that in 1933 Congress adopted the Twenty-First Amendment to repeal the Eighteenth. On December 5, 1933, Utah became the last state needed to approve the amendment, and it once again became legal to drink in the United States. Although Prohibition failed nationally, states began more closely regulating the sale and consumption of alcohol.

Teens and Alcohol

Until Prohibition, there had been few restrictions on drinking and no age limits, which meant teenagers could drink. This was partly because until the twentieth century, many teens began working, marrying, and leaving home to live alone at earlier ages than today. When Prohibition ended in 1933, most states set the drinking age at twenty-one, which was also the voting age at the time. There were some exceptions: Ohio set the drinking age at sixteen before raising it to eighteen in 1935, and Wisconsin and a few other states allowed eighteen-year-olds to drink beer. The differing drinking ages in neighboring states sometimes led young people to cross state lines to drink, often with disastrous results because they had to drive long distances to drink.

In the 1960s Judy was one of seven teenagers who drove more than 100 miles (161km) from Chicago, Illinois, to a community near Milwaukee, Wisconsin, so they could drink; the drinking age in Illinois was twenty-one, but it was only eighteen to drink beer in certain Wisconsin counties. She explains what happened: "Going home the guy driving lost control of the car and we wound up in a ditch. The driver was drunk but we [the passengers] didn't care. We were all pretty much tipsy. No one was injured but we all got arrested and taken into jail. My mother had to come and pick us up."[19] Although Judy and her friends got off lightly, many teens who crossed borders to drink were severely injured or killed in such crashes.

The nation's involvement in the Vietnam War in the 1960s led the nation to amend the U.S. Constitution in 1971 to lower the voting age from 21 to 18. That was because so many young men aged 18 to 20 were fighting and dying for their country. The same reasoning led some thirty states between 1969 and 1976 to lower their drinking ages to 18. Alex Wagenaar, a University of Florida professor who is an expert on alcohol-related issues, explains, "The argument became: If 18 year-olds can fight and vote, then they should be able to have a drink."[20] The decision to allow teens to drink, however, proved disastrous.

ALCOHOL PROMOTES MORAL IMPAIRMENT

"Spirits impair the memory, debilitate the understanding, and pervert the moral faculties . . . produce not only falsehood, but fraud, theft, uncleanliness, and murder."—Benjamin Rush, one of the signers of the Declaration of Independence

Quoted in C. Furnas. *The Life and Times of the Late Demon Rum.* New York: Putnam's Sons, 1965, p. 111.

Between 1970 and 1975 there was a 15 to 20 percent increase in alcohol-related automobile accidents involving teenagers, and

*In 1984 President Ronald Reagan signed legislation that raised the national
drinking age to twenty-one.*

the estimated number of teens who died in such crashes rose from 7,797 to nearly 9,000. The increased danger to teens led eleven states to raise their drinking ages again. The actions by those states to protect teenagers did not completely solve the problem. Again, many teens simply drove across states lines to drink in states where the age was lower. In the end it would require action by the federal government to solve the crisis of teenage drunk drivers.

The National Minimum Drinking Age Act

In 1982 President Ronald Reagan established a commission to study the nation's drunk driving problem. On April 5, 1983, Reagan said the commission had formulated thirty-nine proposals to reduce drunk driving, one of which was to establish a uniform drinking age of twenty-one. Reagan said, "Because of the correlation between the number of drunk driving fatalities and liberal drinking-age laws, the Commission has recommended that every State set twenty-one as the minimum legal age for drinking alcoholic beverages."[21] On July 17, 1984, Congress passed the National Minimum Drinking Age Act to require all states to make age twenty-one the minimum age for purchasing and publicly possessing alcoholic beverages. The act was not mandatory. As an incentive to make states honor the law, the government said it would reduce federal highway funds by 5 percent for any state that did not increase the drinking age by September 1986.

Most states immediately changed their legal drinking age to twenty-one. In January 1985 governors from six northeastern states met in Danbury, Connecticut, and committed themselves to honoring the federal law. New York governor Mario Cuomo explained why he believed a higher drinking age was necessary: "We have people pouring over the borders now from Pennsylvania and the other states [where the age already was twenty-one] coming to us to get a drink because we have 19. That's causing deaths and injury."[22]

Although some states were reluctant to make the change, by 1988 all fifty states had complied with the law and increased their drinking age to twenty-one. One of the strongest public groups backing the change had been Mothers Against Drunk

MADD president Wendy Hamilton (pictured) speaks to the press on the twentieth anniversary of the national law raising the drinking age to twenty-one. Hamilton says the law has saved twenty thousand teens from dying in drunk driving automobile accidents.

Driving (MADD), an organization that has worked hard to make the nation's roads safer by curbing drunk driving. On the twentieth anniversary of the signing of the national age law, MADD president Wendy J. Hamilton praised the effects of the bill. Hamilton said, "Today, 20,000 kids are still living because of that life-changing law. But we can't put the period there. Alcohol is still the number one drug for today's youth."[23]

Why Teens Drink and the Effects of Alcohol

D aniel Radcliffe was eleven years old in 2000 when he won the lead role in *Harry Potter and the Sorcerer's Stone*. In the next decade millions of moviegoers watched Radcliffe grow to adulthood in eight films based on the best-selling novels about the boy wizard written by J.K. Rowling. Like many young people around the world, Radcliffe experimented with alcohol during his teenage years. In an interview in July 2011 before the final Harry Potter movie was released, Radcliffe admitted he was drinking so much by 2008 that his acting suffered when he filmed *Harry Potter and the Half-Blood Prince*. Said Radcliffe: "I became so reliant on [alcohol] to enjoy stuff. There were a few years there when I was just so enamored with the idea of living some sort of famous person's lifestyle that really isn't suited to me."[24] Radcliffe quit drinking in August 2010 when he realized how much alcohol was hurting him.

Radcliffe's reason for drinking—that it was how a world-famous movie star should act—is not one many teenagers can use as an excuse for turning to alcohol. The reasons young people begin drinking, however, are many and varied. Although many young people begin drinking for the same reasons, every teenager has his or her own particular motive for taking that first drink of alcohol.

"A Fact of Life"

In *A Six-Pack and a Fake I.D.*, Susan and Daniel Cohen write that most young people will drink alcohol for the first time before they turn twenty-one. They claim teenage drinking is so widespread that teens consider it an ordinary activity, one that

Harry Potter film star Daniel Radcliffe (pictured) says that during the filming of Harry Potter and the Half-Blood Prince *he relied on alcohol to enjoy life. He quit drinking in August 2010 when he realized how much alcohol was hurting him.*

they and most of their friends feel they have a right to do even though it is illegal: "Drinking—it's a fact of life that you confront in your teen years. You may consider drinking a pleasure, a right, and a social necessity. Your parents, your school, and the over twenty one world in general may consider your drinking a problem—and they have made it illegal to boot. But you're not going to let that stop you!"[25]

It is hard for many teenagers to believe they are doing anything wrong, because in a few years they will be able to drink legally. The fact that many adults in their lives drink alcohol also makes them question why they cannot. It is especially hard for teenagers to think drinking is wrong if their parents or close relatives are heavy drinkers. A recovering alcoholic who chose to use a pseudonym wrote online that his father accidentally conditioned him to believe drinking was a good thing by giving him sips of beer when he was a small child. He wrote that because "my father was always 'happy' when he was drinking [I] quickly equated drinking with happiness."[26]

"BECAUSE I CAN'T"

"Because I can't do it responsibly. Because one drink doesn't relax me; it only energizes me and makes me want more. Because I can't get out of my own way if I drink. Because my life is better sober. Because, towards the end of my drinking, I didn't have a life anymore."—Anna David, author of the novel *Party Girl*, who began drinking at age twelve, explains why she quit

Quoted in Caren Osten Gerszberg. "Interview with Anna David, Author of the Memoir, 'Falling for Me.'" *Drinking Diaries: From Celebration to Revelation*, October 12, 2011. www.drinkingdiaries.com/2011/10/12/interview-with-anna-david-author-of.

Teenagers also have a difficult time rejecting drinking because they are bombarded daily with television commercials, newspaper and magazine advertisements, and billboards extolling the virtues of various brands of beer and alcohol. The media blitz reinforces their belief that drinking is normal. "We Americans live in an alcohol rich environment," James B. Jacobs writes. Jacobs is a law professor who has studied the drunk driving problem in the United States. In *Drunk Driving: An American Dilemma*, Jacobs claims that society's overwhelming acceptance of alcohol is one reason why so many people drink, teens and adults alike. Jacobs also explains that the reasons people start drinking, and then often find it hard to stop, are due to the way alcohol affects people psychologically and emotionally:

Drinkers seek reduction of tension, guilt, anxiety, and frustration. From personal experience and from viewing countless television and movie dramas, we have become accustomed to people turning to alcohol to cope with a hard day, family problems, or bad news. People also imbibe alcohol to loosen up, let down their hair, release inhibitions. [People] also turn to alcohol to fortify confidence, enhance self-esteem, and increase aggressiveness.[27]

The basic psychological and emotional benefits people seek when they drink are common to both teenagers and adults. However, teenagers have their own unique sets of circumstances that can push them toward taking that first sip of alcohol. One of the most powerful is that they are trying to leave childhood behind and gain what they perceive as the exalted status of being an adult.

Reasons Why Teens Drink

Teenagers have many and varied reasons for drinking. In *Teens Under the Influence*, Katherine Ketcham and Nicholas A. Pace list some of the reasons why teenagers drink:

Many kids use drugs for the same general reasons adults use drugs—to get high, to feel happy, stimulated, relaxed, or intoxicated; to ease stress, frustration, tension, disappointment, fear, or anger; to take their minds off their pain or their troubles. Kids may start drinking or using other drugs to impress their friends, to rebel against their parents or society, or because they don't want to be seen as preppies or suck-ups. [They may drink] to fit in, or to avoid drawing attention to themselves. If they belong to a gang, they may use drugs to win respect, be cool, or just because that's what everyone else is doing. [Teens] who are anxious or fearful may use alcohol and/or other drugs to boost their self-confidence. Extroverted, outgoing teenagers may use drugs because they like the company of other fun loving, risk-taking kids.

Katherine Ketcham and Nicholas A. Pace. *Teens Under the Influence: The Truth About Kids, Alcohol, and Other Drugs—How to Recognize the Problem and What to Do About It*. New York: Ballantine, 2003, p. 25.

Adulthood and Peer Pressure

Toren Volkmann did not start drinking heavily until he went to college; when that happened he could not stop and became an alcoholic. After Volkmann managed to quit, he and his mother, Chris, wrote a book about his descent into alcoholism. Toren wrote about why he believes so many young people start drinking: "I think teenagers view alcohol—and I certainly did—as something that's very glamorous."[28] The powerful attraction teenagers have for alcohol and the almost magical qualities they feel it will endow them with are strongly rooted in their desire to become adults.

Teenagers often feel trapped in the twilight zone between childhood and adulthood. Drinking is something they cannot legally do until they are older, so having that first drink becomes a rite of passage to adulthood, like getting a driver's license, going to college, or working to support themselves. Or as Mike explained when he was asked why he began drinking in high school at age sixteen: "It makes you feel like one of the older guys instead of a little kid."[29]

An equally powerful reason teenagers start drinking is peer pressure. Alexandra Robbins wrote *The Geeks Shall Inherit the Earth*, a book that explains why some people who are not popular in high school become successful as adults. Robbins interviewed many young people about their fierce desire to be popular. She said in an interview that peer pressure to conform to accepted standards of conduct among fellow students leads many young people to start drinking so they will be accepted and respected:

> Many surveys report that the average age students begin drinking is about 14. Many students told me that they start to feel pressure to drink in seventh grade. Anecdotally, teens say that they drink to have fun and to let off steam, but mostly to fit in. They think that everyone else is drinking, so they figure they have to conform. Also, they want to prove that there's "more to them" than what classmates see at school. They figure if they drink, that proves that they can party.[30]

One of the big reasons teenagers drink is peer pressure. Pressure to conform to the accepted standards of conduct among their peer group leads many teenagers to start drinking so they will be socially accepted.

Behavioral psychologist Reid K. Hester wrote an online article for *Selfhelp Magazine* about why teenagers drink. On February 18, 2011, a reader who identified himself only as "Texas" posted an online comment on the article in which he gave his own explanation of why junior and senior high school students drink: "Teenagers drink because they are a part of an age group that is a part of a social group that drinks. It's popular to have fun, that's a common fact. [There] is also the fact that it's not allowed so it kind of gives it that rebellious factor."[31] The same need to fit in and be liked can also lead older teenagers to start drinking. It happened to Volkmann when he left home to attend college: "At college, you'll encounter a whole new group of people, many of [whom] drink regularly. I got sucked into that very lifestyle, and after a while, I found it did me no good. There is so much pressure to drink not only from your friends, but to just fit in when you go off to college."[32]

Wanting to act like an adult and peer pressure are the two main reasons young people start drinking. But teenagers, like adults, also drink alcohol because of how it makes them feel.

Changing How They Feel

Most people like to drink because of the powerful effect it has on their emotions. Hester, who has studied the effects of alcohol on teens, explains how alcohol can affect people: "Alcohol is a powerful drug and changes how you feel. Some of the initial sensations at lower blood alcohol levels are pleasant and it is this sensation that many teens, as well as adults, seek. . . . If you're tense or uptight, drinking some alcohol will, at least initially, reduce some of that tension and help you 'chill out.'"[33]

"MAYBE I WAS BORED"

"I don't know why I did it. It wasn't peer pressure . . . a lot of my friends don't drink at all. My parents don't drink. [Mostly] I drank hard liquor. Maybe I was bored. It was a small town, and it seemed like there wasn't anything else to do."—Michelle, who began drinking heavily on weekends at age eighteen and later quit, does not know why she started

Quoted in Barbara Strauch. *The Primal Teen: What the New Discoveries About the Teenage Brain Tell Us About Our Kids.* New York: Doubleday, 2003, p. 174.

Other drugs like marijuana, cocaine, and heroin create similar mood changes. But alcohol is easier for teenagers to get, so it is usually their first choice to get high, the feeling of euphoria that can accompany drinking. Teenagers are especially vulnerable to wanting to feel better, or at least different, because of the tremendous changes taking place in their lives, including the anxieties of dating and learning to socialize with other young people. Jeff drank for the first time at age thirteen when he took a bottle of his father's liquor and shared it with a friend. He said he learned to like drinking because it made him feel good and made him more comfortable in social situations: "It made me feel good. All my anxiety and shyness left and I could talk to girls and other people and dance at parties with no nervousness. It definitely helped me feel more at ease. I was more outgoing when drinking. I did start going to more parties when drinking because I was socially more comfortable when drunk."[34]

Wendy began drinking so she could fit in at school: "I never felt like I belonged anywhere. [But] I could be whoever I wanted to be when I was drinking."[35] Wendy had her first drink when she was twelve, and her first heavy drinking experience came a year later during her first date when she went to a dance. When other students passed around a bottle of whiskey, she drank so much that she became violently ill. But Wendy liked how alcohol made her feel and continued drinking despite that first awful experience.

"LIQUID COURAGE"

"Alcohol makes me feel good, you know, happy, crazy, full of myself. It gives me liquid courage—I feel I can do anything. I don't always like myself when I'm sober. But after a few six-packs I feel much better about myself."—Thomas, who was locked up in a juvenile detention center and had been arrested a dozen times on various criminal charges during his teenage years

Quoted in Katherine Ketcham and Nicholas A. Pace. *Teens Under the Influence: The Truth About Kids, Alcohol, and Other Drugs—How to Recognize the Problem and What to Do About It*. New York: Ballantine, 2003, pp. 3–4.

Being more comfortable socially is one of the many reasons teens drink. Another reason is to ease their emotional turmoil over a wide range of problems. Anger motivated John to begin drinking at age fifteen. After his parents divorced, John had become close to his grandfather. His grandfather's death made him so angry that he began drinking to feel better: "I was angry that he was taken away. I didn't understand. I was lonely. I was a latchkey kid. I just started doing stuff because I was so angry, I think."[36] *The Kids Are All Right* is both an autobiographical book

Alcohol is a powerful drug that changes how one feels. Moderate drinking tends to lead to feelings of euphoria and a reduction of tension.

and movie about what happened to Amanda, Liz, Diana, and Dan Welch after both their parents died in just a few years. In 1985, when their mom died three years after their dad, nineteen-year-old Amanda said she and sixteen-year-old Liz turned to alcohol to relieve their depression: "We often escaped the sadness by partying."[37]

The emotional changes alcohol creates in drinkers is this powerful drug's main attraction. The reason alcohol can make people feel different is how it works in their bodies.

Unhappy teens suffering from depression often turn to alcohol to relieve the symptoms.

How Alcohol Works

In a book on alcoholism, James R. Milam and Katherine Ketcham write that alcohol is not only a powerful, dangerous, and sometimes deadly drug but also one that is mystifying in how it affects people: "Alcohol is an infinitely confusing substance. In small amounts it is an exhilarating stimulant. In larger amounts it acts as a sedative and as a toxin, or poisonous agent. When taken in very large amounts over long periods of time [it] can be damaging to cells, tissues, and organs."[38]

When people drink, their bodies begin absorbing alcohol immediately—5 to 10 percent of alcohol is transferred to the bloodstream directly through the lining of the mouth. After a person swallows a sip of beer, wine, or liquor, the stomach and small intestine speedily absorb the alcohol. The first small doses of alcohol increase blood flow, accelerate the heart rate, and stimulate brain cells to speed up the transmission of nerve impulses. This is due to the calories alcohol contains, which, as food, make the body feel good. Those simple physical changes can ease emotional tension and make people feel happier. Alcohol also makes people feel good because small doses of it boost levels of dopamine, a neurotransmitter in the brain related to pleasurable sensations.

However, the effects alcohol has on people change as they continue drinking. It is then that alcohol reveals its true nature as a powerful central nervous system depressant, one that is generally classified with drugs such as barbiturates, minor tranquilizers, and general anesthetics. As a depressant, alcohol depresses —slows down—operation of the central nervous system, which includes the brain and the spinal cord. Depressed performance of the central nervous system from alcohol consumption creates the slurred speech, impaired physical coordination, and other physical and mental symptoms of intoxication.

A standard drink is defined as one that contains 0.5 ounces (14g) of alcohol. Because of their varying alcohol contents, that amount of alcohol is found in 12 ounces (340g) of beer, 5 ounces (141.7g) of wine, or 1.5 ounces (42.5g) of 80-proof distilled spirits such as whiskey or vodka. The human body can process alcohol at a fixed rate of one drink per hour, so people who consume more than one drink per hour will have increasingly high levels of alcohol in their blood. The level of intoxication drinkers experience is linked to the body's blood alcohol concentration (BAC), the amount of alcohol in the blood measured in percentages. A BAC of 0.10 percent means a person's bloodstream has 1 part alcohol per 1,000 parts of blood. A BAC of 0.08 percent is legal proof in every state that a person is drunk.

People become intoxicated because alcohol affects their brain, which controls their physical functioning as well as their emotions. The speed and severity with which people become intoxicated depends on several other factors besides how much alcohol they drink or how fast they consume it. One is the size of the drinker. Someone weighing 250 pounds (113.4kg) will not become as drunk by the same amount of alcohol as someone weighing 125 pounds (56.7kg); their blood supply is correspondingly bigger, so their BAC will not rise as rapidly as that of a smaller person drinking the same amount of alcohol. People who have eaten recently or eat while they drink absorb alcohol more slowly because their body is absorbing food as well as alcohol. Women generally metabolize alcohol more quickly than men, which means they can become intoxicated more quickly. Some people are also able to drink more without being affected by alcohol because of their unique body chemistry.

Teenagers are more susceptible to the effects of alcohol if they are drinking for the first time or have not drunk alcohol very often. Adults who drink regularly develop a tolerance for alcohol that lessens its effects on them. Young people are also

The same amount of alcohol is contained in 12 ounces of beer, 5 ounces of wine, or 1.5 ounces of 80-proof liquor.

less experienced than adults in handling the physical and emotional effects alcohol causes in drinkers.

Thus, different people become drunk at different rates. Although alcohol's effects on drinkers are similar, they are also many and varied, and they change as people keep drinking.

The Effects of Being Drunk

BAC levels determine how drunk someone is. As BAC increases, so do the symptoms of intoxication. In *A Six-Pack and a Fake I.D.*, authors Susan and Daniel Cohen explain the basic effects alcohol has on people at various BACs: "Alcohol alters the way you think and move. By 0.10 percent, speech is slurred. By 0.15 percent [people] have trouble walking. By 0.30 percent, people might start throwing up and becoming confused and unaware of where they are. At 0.40 percent, people start passing out and [this is] also the level that can kill someone."[39]

At its highest levels, alcohol acts as a poison that can kill drinkers by depressing their brain activity so much that they stop breathing. This form of death is known as alcohol poisoning. This can happen because alcohol affects the brain more strongly than any other part of the body. The brain's fatty material readily absorbs alcohol when the bloodstream delivers it, which means that there is truth in the saying "That drink went right to my head."

Alcohol that hits a person's brain affects not only how it controls the body physically but also how the drinker will react mentally and emotionally. Harry Milt, author of *Alcoholism, Its Causes and Cure: A New Handbook*, explains that this impairment sneaks up on people as they keep drinking: "With the first drink or two an illusion may be created of clarity of mind and thought [but] as the alcohol continues to bathe the brain, consciousness becomes blurred, thinking is slowed down, the content of thought is [reduced], memory is blurred. Concepts are poorly formulated, reasoning is foggy, judgment is blunted."[40]

Higher levels of alcohol can cause emotional changes in drinkers, including making them angry over small things that happen, which is why fights in bars are common. Alcohol also reduces natural inhibitions that keep people from doing dangerous

How Does Alcohol Make People Feel Good?

The main reason people drink is that alcohol makes them feel good. When their bloodstream channels alcohol to the brain, it affects the nucleus accumbens. This specialized part of the brain is the seat of emotion and pleasure that is responsible for feelings of gratification, such as when people eat to satisfy hunger. When alcohol and other addictive drugs hit the nucleus accumbens, the nucleus accumbens releases dopamine, which produces feelings ranging from mild happiness to euphoria. *Newsweek* reporter Sharon Begley explains how this works:

"Drugs of abuse increase the concentration of dopamine in the brain's reward circuits," says Nora Volkow of Brookhaven National Lab. The drugs do that more intensely than any mere behavior, be it eating a four-star meal or winning the lottery.[Dopamine] produces a feel-good sensation. Eating cheesecake or tacos or any other food you love activates it. So does winning a competition, acing a test, receiving praise and other pleasurable experiences. The pleasure circuit communicates in the chemical language of dopamine: this neurotransmitter zips from neuron to neuron in the circuit like a molecular happy face.

Sharon Begley. "How It All Starts in Your Brain." *Newsweek*, February 12, 2001, p. 40.

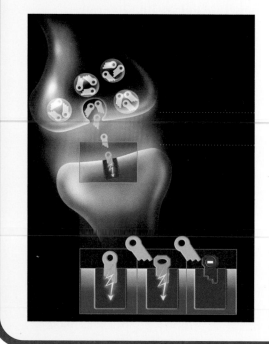

An illustration of a nerve synapse. When alcohol enters the nucleus accumbens it causes the release of dopamine (seen crossing the neuron), which produces feelings from mild happiness to euphoria.

Alcohol reduces natural inhibitions that keep people from engaging in risky behaviors they would never consider while sober.

or foolish things. People who are drunk may engage in dangerous activities they would never consider when they are sober, such as car surfing, being promiscuous, or driving when they know they have had too much to drink. This happens because large amounts of alcohol destroy people's ability to understand what is happening to them physically, intellectually, and emotionally.

One of the effects of drinking too much is that intoxicated people usually do not realize how severely alcohol has affected them. For example, when eighteen-year-old Keaton Leon Hannah was arrested on June 17, 2011, in Verdigris, Oklahoma, a Verdigris police officer claims he heard Hannah say, "I'm sorry I didn't realize I was so drunk."[41] Drinking had robbed Hannah of the ability to understand how severely alcohol had impaired his ability to drive and to make good decisions.

DANGERS FOR TEEN DRINKERS

Chris likes to skateboard. But, when the sixteen-year-old drinks, he believes he can do dangerous maneuvers or tricks he would not attempt when sober. Chris once had a spectacular crash and was knocked out when he tried to skate down a long, steep flight of one hundred stairs. In talking about the accident, Chris seemed unconcerned about the risk he had taken: "I broke a couple teeth, knocked myself out, got cuts and scraped everything—for a while there, I was really flying. It was amazing."[42]

Chris's blasé attitude toward such risky behavior can be partly understood by the fact that alcohol dulls inhibitions. However, some adults believe that teenagers often make poor decisions in dangerous situations whether alcohol is involved or not, because teenagers do not think about the life-threatening risks they take. Now there is some scientific evidence to support this belief. In recent years scientists have learned that teenagers may take more unnecessary risks than adults because the part of their brain that assesses danger is not fully developed. Chuck Nelson is a professor of pediatrics at Harvard Medical School who has studied how human brains develop. Nelson humorously explains this teenage structural brain weakness by saying, "Basically, this is the part [of the brain] that tells you to count to ten before you call your mother old and stupid."[43]

The Teenage Brain

Scientists who study the brain have known for a long time that the brains of six-year-olds are 95 percent the size they will be when the children are adults. In the past, scientists believed that because the brain was so large by then, it was mostly done developing and

Teenagers are prone to making poor decisions in dangerous situations regardless of whether alcohol is involved, because they have a lower impulse control than adults.

changing. More recent studies, however, have proved that the brain is still undergoing complex changes when people are in their early twenties. Some of the most important changes happen in the frontal lobe, the part of the brain that helps people resist impulses and make good decisions.

Deborah Yurgelun-Todd, a neuroscientist at McLean Hospital in Belmont, Massachusetts, has studied how teenage brains influence teens' reactions to various situations. She believes the unfinished development of the frontal lobes of teenage brains makes it harder for teenagers to see the potential consequences of their behavior. Yurgelun-Todd claims this incomplete development leads teenagers to act impulsively without properly assessing dangers involved in situations they encounter:

> To appreciate what the consequences of a behavior are, you have to really think through what the potential outcomes of a behavior are. I think the frontal lobe . . . is not always functioning fully in teenagers. That would suggest that teenagers aren't thinking through what the consequences of their behaviors are [and] they're not going to be so worried about whether or not what they're doing has a negative consequence.[44]

Examples of risky teenage decisions are those that high school student Vanessa makes about how she interacts with students. Vanessa knows she should be careful about wandering

A doctor describes the teen brain at the National Institutes of Health. The unfinished development of the frontal lobes of teenage brains makes it harder for them to perceive the consequences of their behavior.

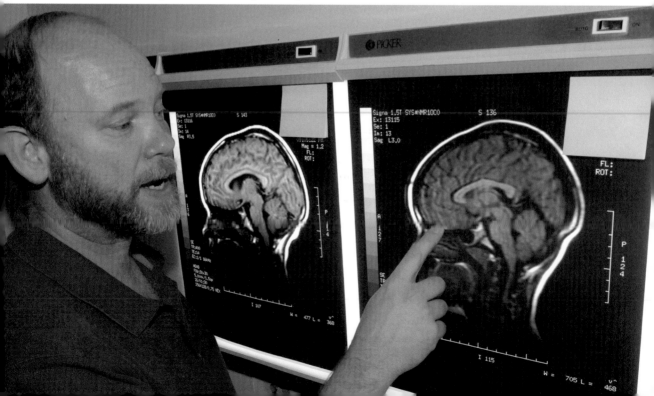

into the wrong section of the cafeteria because different groups of students control different areas. But Vanessa admits she likes taking "emotional risks" and that "sometimes I actually like doing that. I want to rebel against the way things are. . . . I want to do that just to see what happens."[45]

ALCOHOL AND THE TEENAGE BRAIN

"Adolescents and adults respond in different ways to the same amount of alcohol. Compared to adults, adolescents tend to be less sensitive to alcohol's calming effect, and they are less sensitive to alcohol's effects on motor coordination. But when it comes to reasoning, logic, and memory—skills controlled by different brain structures—adolescents are much more vulnerable to alcohol-induced impairment."—Authors Katherine Ketcham and Nicholas A. Pace

Katherine Ketcham and Nicholas A. Pace. *Teens Under the Influence: The Truth About Kids, Alcohol, and Other Drugs—How to Recognize the Problem and What to Do About It.* New York: Ballantine, 2003, p. 44.

When alcohol is added to a teenage brain already weak in making decisions, the results can be disastrous. The first bad decision teenagers make is to drink, because it is illegal for them just to have alcohol. Getting alcohol, however, is not very hard for many teens.

Punished for Having Alcohol

Teenagers have to obtain alcohol illegally. Sometimes it is as easy as finding a store that sells alcohol to teenagers. When Jack was in high school, he discovered a liquor store that would sell him beer. Jack regularly went to the store and bought six packs for his friends. He says he did it because "it made me a cool guy, a big time guy. That helped me be part of the group."[46] Many teens get older friends or siblings to buy alcohol for them, and some purchase it themselves with fake identification. Jeff, who at seventeen looked older than he was, says he "got a fake ID that one of my friends made for me. I used it to buy beer at convenience

Taking Risks Is Normal

In *The Primal Teen: What the New Discoveries About the Teenage Brain Tell Us About Our Kids*, author Barbara Strauch writes that trying new things, even if it involves some risks, is part of growing up for teenagers:

> Many child psychologists say human teenagers [need] to do chancy things to find out who they are, where they fit in. And parents need to figure out when the chancy thing is within normal range and when its moved far beyond—a tricky calculation that can often depend on the kids themselves. For some kids, trying out for the school play or taking an advanced math class is all the risk they need. For others, it's flying over ravines on mountain bikes, walking on the wild side of town, or taking the first gulp of beer. [Some psychologists] say that teenagers who do experiment in a wide range of areas—even drugs and alcohol in a limited way—often adjust better in the long run than those who completely hold themselves back.

Barbara Strauch. *The Primal Teen: What the New Discoveries About the Teenage Brain Tell Us About Our Kids*. New York: Doubleday, 2003, p. 89.

For some teens, risk may mean taking an advanced math class or trying out for a school play. For others it may be flying over rough terrain on mountain bikes or taking their first drink of beer.

stores. I never got caught using the fake ID."[47] Teens also steal alcohol, from their parents or the homes of people they know. In an online interview about drinking, L*anne St*kes explained what happened when she took some vodka: "I stole some Smirnoff from an older married couple [her parents] I was living with at the time. I mixed it with OJ [orange juice] and remember swaying back and forth like a fall leaf just about to glide off the branch. My ten-year-old sister asked, 'Are you drunk?' 'Noooooo!' I slurred in her face at a decibel so loud an AK 47 fires softer."[48]

DRINKING CULTURE IN COLLEGE

"In high school, it needs to be hidden from parents. In the working world, it must be downplayed to bosses, or concerned friends, or lovers. But in college, we can wear our alcohol abuse as proudly as our university sweatshirt; the two concepts are virtually synonymous."—Koren Zailckas, author of *Smashed: Story of a Drunken Girlhood*, on how young people accept heavy drinking as part of college life

Quoted in Anna Mundow. "The Lost Years of a 'Dead-Drunk Daughter.'" *Irish Times*, February 23, 2005. www.irishtimes.com/newspaper/features/2005/0223/1107916262 150.html.

However teenagers obtain alcohol, they risk being punished just for being caught with it in their possession. Greg began drinking when he was twelve and in the seventh grade. He drank often even though he got into trouble several times. Greg once packed a bottle of vodka in his suitcase when he and some eighth-grade friends went to a cottage his parents owned during summer vacation. When his older sister found the bottle and told his father, his dad came up with an unusual punishment: "He made me and my friends go to mass everyday at 7:15 A.M. under threat of telling everyone's parents if they did not show up. That was quite a way to spend the last two weeks of summer vacation." Police also caught Greg and some friends with alcohol: "Another time the cops found me and some friends drinking beer in a van at a park. We weren't drunk and they were just going to take the beer and let us go but one of our friends made a run for it so they took us all in."[49]

Perhaps the worst place to get caught with alcohol is school. Schools ban alcohol and other drugs, and school officials punish students who are caught drinking or with alcohol in school. In March 2011 a sixth-grade student was punished for bringing a bottle of soda spiked with vodka to Mary Moore Elementary School in Arlington, Texas, and passing it around so his friends could try it. Such incidents occur more often in high school, with prom nights the most typical time that students drink at school. In May 2011 a large group of students showed up drunk at a prom at Methacton Area High School in Eagleville, Pennsylvania. Forty-one students were suspended from school for two to ten days and required to perform up to twenty hours of community service such as cleaning graffiti from buildings. Student athletes caught drinking were also suspended from their teams for fifteen days.

Such punishments, however, seem minor compared to what can happen to teenagers who drink. All too often teens become seriously ill from drinking, or worse, die from alcohol poisoning.

Binge Drinking and Drugs

Fourteen-year-old Takeimi Rao of Santa Rosa, California, died on July 10, 2011, after she and three friends drank vodka during a sleepover. They also became violently ill but survived. Although an autopsy was inconclusive, it was believed Rao died because she drank more alcohol than her body could handle. Teenagers often do not understand how toxic large amounts of alcohol can be. Each year about two hundred thousand girls and boys are taken to emergency rooms in the United States after drinking enough to become violently ill. Peak times for such visits are New Year's Eve, other holidays, and summer vacation.

Most medical emergencies involving alcohol occur during binge drinking sessions. The Centers for Disease Control and Prevention (CDC) has stated that more than 90 percent of the alcohol that drinkers age twelve to twenty consume is during such drinking bouts. The National Institute on Alcohol Abuse and Alcoholism (NIAAA) has defined a *binge* as a session in which someone drinks enough to raise his or her BAC to 0.08 percent or higher. To reach that level, a male has to consume five or more drinks and a female four in about two hours. However, many teens often drink enough to reach far higher levels—and the higher the level, the sicker they become.

On March 13, 2011, nineteen-year-old Molly Ammon was found dead after a night of drinking with friends in Madeira Beach, Florida. The University of Florida freshman had a BAC of 0.408 percent. High school friend Meredith Kelley was devastated over Ammon's death because Ammon was so well liked: "Molly showed us all how to laugh at ourselves. She had such energy. Everyone wanted to be near her."[50] Kelley flew home from college in Colorado to attend her friend's funeral.

Each year approximately two hundred thousand teens are taken to emergency rooms after drinking enough to become violently ill.

Ammon's death was not unusual. The NIAAA estimates that at least fourteen hundred college students die annually from alcohol-related causes, including about four hundred from alcohol poisoning. The NIAA believes heavy drinking among college students, most of them younger than twenty-one, is due to a culture of alcohol use that has developed over many years: "Customs that promote college drinking . . . are embedded in numerous levels of students' environments. . . . Environmental and peer influences combine to create a culture of drinking. This culture actively promotes drinking, or passively promotes it, through tolerance, or even tacit approval, of college drinking as a rite of passage."[51]

Binge drinking among college students often includes games like Beeropoly, which is patterned after the board game Monopoly and requires players to drink beer. Other games involve shots of liquor, which, because of the high alcohol content, make participants drunk more quickly. Younger teens also play such games. Some college fraternities and campus groups force new members to drink large quantities of alcohol as part of initiation rites before accepting them as new members.

DO NOT DRINK, PERIOD

"I think society has taught kids so well to not drink and drive. But they don't realize that it can be dangerous to drink and stay at home."—Angie Ammon, after her nineteen-year-old daughter, Molly, died of alcohol poisoning on March 13, 2011

Quoted in Jessica Vander Velde. "UF Freshman from Tampa Found Dead by Friends in Madeira Beach Condo." *St. Petersburg (FL) Times*, March 15, 2011. www.tampabay.com/news/publicsafety/uf-freshman-from-tampa-found-dead-by-friends-in-madeira-beach-condo/1157270a.

Another dangerous thing teens do is mix alcohol with other drugs, including prescription drugs, which are often stolen from home. Seventeen-year-old Rob explains why teens enjoy doing this: "It's like a science experiment. You drink alcohol and then take some Ecstacy, pop some OxyContin, or smoke some marijuana and

The National Institute on Drug Abuse's director Nora Volkow warns teens that mixing alcohol with OxyContin, Xanax, Valium, Vicodin, and other drugs is extremely dangerous.

wait to see what happens. Sometimes its just a nice mellow buzz—but sometimes its like an explosion and just gone—you feel completely out of it. It's weird because you never know exactly what's going to happen."[52]

Mixing other drugs with alcohol is popular, but Nora Volkow, director of the National Institute on Drug Abuse, warns that mixing alcohol with OxyContin, Vicodin, Xanax, Valium, and other drugs is extremely dangerous. Volkow said because teenagers do not know how a mixture of drugs and alcohol will affect them, they are "playing a game of Russian roulette they don't understand."[53] These mixtures can result in serious sickness, hospitalization, and death.

ALCOHOL TAKES OVER

"You don't just wake up one day and say 'What happened?' I mean, it just slowly takes over your life. You don't know that it's beginning to take a priority, except one day you wake up and you know you've got to have it, because you can't function [without it]. But then it fools you, because you know you only need to take the one, but then you take that one, and, boom, you want more."—Wendy, on how she became an alcoholic at sixteen

Quoted in Janet Firshein. "Wendy: Freedom to Drink, or Freedom to Live?" Thirteen.org. www.thirteen.org/closetohome/stories/html/wendy.html.

The deaths of the two young women mentioned above are typical of the dangers teenagers face when they binge drink. Their deaths also highlight the fact that young women face more dangers than their male counterparts when they drink heavily.

Dangers for Teenage Girls

Mark Willenbring, a doctor with the NIAAA, said women should be even more careful than men when they drink because they usually weigh less and their bodies absorb alcohol differently than men's bodies. Both factors mean that if a woman drinks the same amount of alcohol as a man, she will likely become drunk more quickly. Willenbring said women are especially at risk if they participate in drinking games that force them to quickly drink a lot of alcohol: "We're absolutely seeing more women competing in drinking games. That's a terribly dangerous thing to do."[54]

Alcohol can make women pass out or become ill more easily because it affects them so strongly. Amanda Welch and her siblings wrote *The Kids Are All Right*. She explains what happened to her sixteen-year-old sister, Liz, when she drank too much in Brooklyn, New York: "One night, Liz and I met some friends at a club and Liz got completely wasted. One minute, we were doing tequila shots, the next, she was nowhere in sight. I finally found her hours later, curled up in a ball on the floor of the men's room."[55]

Another significant danger that women face when getting drunk is being sexually assaulted. It is estimated that ninety-seven thousand college students each year are victims of alcohol-related sexual assault or date rape. The Rape, Abuse and Incest National Network claims that one in six women will be victims of sexual assault during their lifetime. The group also says girls aged sixteen to nineteen are four times more likely

It has been estimated that every year 97,000 female college students are victims of alcohol-related sexual assault or date rape.

than women in any other age group to be victims of rape, attempted rape, or sexual assault. Alcohol is a common factor in sexual assault because women who are drunk are easy prey for boyfriends or strangers who want to have sex even if their victims do not.

On June 22, 2011, an eighteen-year-old girl testified about being raped by a thirty-two-year-old Uniontown, Pennsylvania, man two years earlier when she was sixteen. She testified in court that on June 21, 2009, she and her boyfriend had been drinking heavily and taking prescription drugs at the man's home. After her boyfriend passed out, the man assaulted her; she was too drunk to stop him. She asked the man in court during the trial: "How could you have taken something from me that wasn't yours to take? I laid there as you took what little self-esteem I had left, looking at the clock, begging the minutes to go faster."[56]

In 2006 the Women's Center of Tarrant County, Texas, warned young women about the danger of drinking and unwanted sex after several teenage girls in Dallas were sexually assaulted in incidents involving alcohol. Deborah Gardner, a spokesperson for the group, said when a woman is intoxicated she cannot give permission to someone to have sex. She also stressed that such incidents are not the victim's fault: "People make mistakes all the time, and we put ourselves in vulnerable situations all the time. But it doesn't justify someone else's faulty thinking or their deviancy."[57]

Alcohol creates special dangers for women and teenage girls. However, both male and female teenage drinkers face health threats that adults do not.

Teen Alcohol Problems

Because teenage brains are still developing, alcohol affects them differently than it does adult brains. Duke University psychiatry professor Aaron White has written studies about the effects of heavy drinking by college students: "There is no doubt about it now: there are long-term cognitive consequences to excessive drinking of alcohol in adolescence."[58] One study showed that teens who had consumed at least two drinks a day for two years were able to remember 10 percent less on memory tests than nondrinking teenagers. That memory weakness was large enough to make it harder for students to pass tests requiring memorization. Such damage to the way the brain operates, however, is not the only way alcohol hurts teenage brains. Joseph A. Califano Jr., founder of Columbia University's National Center on Addiction and Substance Abuse, states, "Alcohol damages the young brain, interferes with mental and social development, and interrupts academic progress."[59]

Wendy, who had her first drink at age twelve, is an example of a teen whose life was nearly destroyed by alcohol. When Wendy began drinking regularly in high school, she liked it so

A study has shown that teens who consume at least two drinks a day for two years remember 10 percent less on memory tests than nondrinking teenagers.

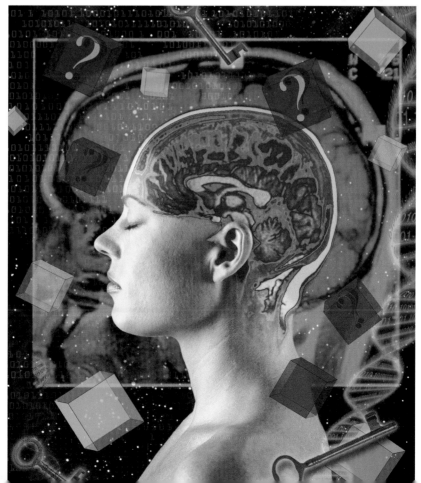

A College Alcoholic

Richard Carriero became an alcoholic during his college years. In 2006, five years after he quit drinking, Carriero wrote about how easily alcohol gained control of his life:

I drank only a handful of times throughout my tenure in high school. When [I went to college] I was fully armed with a strong awareness of what drugs and alcohol can do to a person. I was armed as an 18 year old can be against the pitfalls of peer pressure.

It all went out the window within months of the beginning of my freshman year. . . . I wanted friends, I wanted to have fun and enjoy the freedom of being away from home. I went to parties and made friends. Before I knew it I was drinking 3–4 days a week. Within 9 months I was smoking cigarettes and marijuana as well. . . . Each drink or drag that I took which didn't kill me undermined years of what I was taught until I had no faith left in what I had learned from my family or my education. This was how alcohol got a hold of me—very gradually.

Richard Carriero. "Experiences of a Young Alcoholic: Reflections After Five Years of Sobriety." Associated Content, December 13, 2006. www.associatedcontent.com/article/97635/experiences_of_a_young_alcoholic_reflections.html?cat=5.

much that she quit going to school at sixteen so she could drink all the time. The freedom to party all the time was fun until alcohol began causing serious problems. One time when Wendy was drunk, she stood on a window ledge of a Brooklyn brownstone to attract attention from a boyfriend; she almost died when she fell four stories to the ground. She also sliced both sides of her face with a razor blade once when she was drunk.

The problem for Wendy was that she had become an alcoholic and could not stop drinking for many years. Although Wendy was eventually able to stop drinking as an adult, she said the period in which she felt she had to keep drinking was terrible: "It's insanity that happens when you're in the throes of this disease because the things you're doing are inhuman. You're lying, you're cheating. . . . I didn't want to cut myself up; I didn't want to jump out windows."[60] And although not everyone who drinks becomes an alcoholic, evidence shows that people who start drinking in their teens have a far greater chance of becoming an alcoholic.

A 2006 study showed that 47 percent of people who began drinking alcohol before age fourteen became alcohol dependent at some time in their lives; that figure compared with just 9 percent of people who did not drink until they were twenty-one. Since only about 10 percent of people become alcoholics, the risk of becoming one is almost five times greater for teenage drinkers. William Damon, director of the Stanford Center on Adolescence, states, "The data is quite clear about teen drinking and it has nothing to do with being puritanical. The earlier a kid starts drinking, the more likely they are to have problems with alcohol in their life."[61]

Alcoholics or even people who just drink heavily suffer severe consequences for the stupid, often harmful things they may do to themselves and others. Thomas is a teen who had been arrested many times on charges related to alcohol. While locked up in a juvenile detention center, he once said that even though he still loved drinking, he hated how it was ruining his life:

> I feel ashamed because of the people I've hurt and the stupid things I've done and the way I've let my family down. I'm the outcast of the family. They don't trust me anymore. I thought loving someone meant that you forgive them and trust them, but maybe I've broken my parents' trust so often that they just cant believe me anymore. It's hard to live with yourself when you feel like you're letting everyone down, like you're a failure in everything you do. You know what I mean?[62]

DRINKING AND DRIVING

On June 15, 2011, eighteen-year-old Carter Womick graduated from Salem High School in Virginia Beach, Virginia. That night Womick hosted a graduation party at his home that lasted into the early morning hours of June 16. What started out as one of the happiest nights of Womick's life ended in tragedy. When Womick decided to drive to a nearby convenience store to buy cigarettes at 3:30 A.M., fifteen-year-old Meghan Gerety accompanied him as a passenger. Not far from his home, Womick lost control of his car while speeding around a curve and crashed into a tree. Both teenagers were hospitalized with injuries; Gerety suffered severe head injuries but survived.

Womick was charged with driving under the influence and possession of alcohol. Tim Sweeny, Womick's childhood friend, admitted, "We like to have fun here or there, but I think he may have gotten carried away. I don't think he generally drives under the influence."[63] However, news reports noted that in April, police had issued Womick a citation for alcohol possession. He paid an eighty-six-dollar fine, but a judge decided not to suspend his driver's license for six months even though state law recommended it. Instead, the judge placed Womick on probation and deferred further action until a later date.

Only nine days before his drunk driving incident, newspapers around the nation had carried stories in which American Automobile Association (AAA) official Justin McNaull called the period between Memorial Day and Labor Day, when most students are on summer vacation, "the hundred deadliest days for teen drivers and teen passengers."[64] McNaull was concerned because teenagers have the highest rate of death and injury in auto accidents of any age group. During the summer months when teens have more free time, they have even more accidents than usual. And when alcohol is involved, as in the Virginia Beach crash, driving becomes extremely dangerous for teenagers.

Teens and Traffic Accidents

Even when teenage drivers have not been drinking, they pose more of a danger to themselves and their passengers than older drivers because they are involved in so many accidents. In 2009 eight teens between the ages of sixteen to nineteen died every day from motor vehicle injuries, and statistics showed that for every mile teens drove, they were four times more likely than older drivers to be involved in a collision. A National Highway Traffic Safety Administration (NHTSA) report sums up how hazardous teen driving is:

> Motor vehicle crashes are the leading cause of death for 15- to 20-year-olds, causing roughly one-third of all deaths for this age group. Teenagers are overrepresented in traffic crashes both as drivers and as passengers. On the basis of miles driven, teenagers are involved in three times as many fatal crashes as all other drivers. The high crash-involvement rate for this age group is caused primarily by their lack of maturity and driving experience coupled with their overconfidence and risk-taking behaviors.[65]

The risk of being involved in an accident is directly linked to how many miles people drive. During the summer months, most teenagers have more free time because they are out of school. A study by Liberty Mutual, an insurance company, and Students Against Destructive Decisions (SADD) reported that during the summer, teenagers drive 44 percent more on average. Thus, during the summer they are involved in more accidents, and more teens wind up injured or dead. Statistics compiled by AAA show that from 2005 to 2009, more than 7,300 drivers and passengers aged 16 to 19 were killed in crashes between Memorial Day and Labor Day. Teen deaths during the summer averaged 442 per month, compared to an average of 363 teen deaths in non-summer months.

AAA official McNaull noted that during the summer teens usually "ride with passengers on what we call 'purposeless trips.'"[66] For teenagers, however, those "purposeless trips" have a purpose. Instead of driving with a specific destination—to the store to buy something, to the doctor for a medical exam, or to the library to get a book—they were driving around with the express purpose of trying to have some fun, even if it was just to cruise and joke around with friends. But since drinking is also part of having fun for many teenagers, alcohol is a major factor in the increased number of auto accidents and fatalities teens have during the summer.

In 2009 eight teenagers died every day from injuries incurred from car accidents. Statistics show that for every mile driven, teens are four times more likely than older drivers to be involved in a collision.

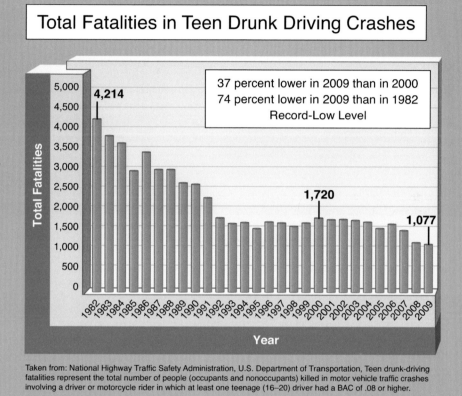

Total Fatalities in Teen Drunk Driving Crashes

37 percent lower in 2009 than in 2000
74 percent lower in 2009 than in 1982
Record-Low Level

4,214

1,720

1,077

Total Fatalities

Year

Taken from: National Highway Traffic Safety Administration, U.S. Department of Transportation, Teen drunk-driving fatalities represent the total number of people (occupants and nonoccupants) killed in motor vehicle traffic crashes involving a driver or motorcycle rider in which at least one teenage (16–20) driver had a BAC of .08 or higher.

U.S. Department of Transportation data for 2009 show that 1,180 teenagers died in drunk driving crashes that year. The good news is that the number of teen deaths involving drunk driving has declined 74 percent since the federal government began tracking such fatalities in 1982, when 4,511 teens died in such crashes, and 38 percent since 2000, when there were 1,710 teen fatalities. The bad news is that so many teenagers still die in alcohol-related crashes.

The Teen Drunk Brain

One reason teens who drink and drive are more likely to be involved in accidents is that alcohol affects their brains differently than it does those of adults. Alcohol is a depressant—people

Drunk teenagers with their impaired judgement, often make poor, alcohol influenced decisions, including driving drunk.

who drink enough alcohol eventually get sleepy and pass out. Alcohol, however, does not sedate teenage brains as much as it does those of adults. Scott Swartzelder, a professor with the Duke University Institute for Brain Sciences, claims this difference has a disastrous effect for teens who drink and drive: "If teenagers don't feel sleepy after they drink, they may think it's OK to get behind the wheel [of a car]."[67] Jack London, one of the early twentieth century's most famed American authors, was an alcoholic. He wrote a book about his drinking called *John Barleycorn: Alcoholic Memoirs*. In that book, he noted that when he was a teenage sailor he was able to keep drinking long after his older companions had fallen asleep.

Due to older age, most adults get very tired when they are drunk and tend to pass out. Teenagers have more natural energy and can stay awake longer while drunk. This gives them more time to make bad, alcohol-influenced decisions. At that point, another of alcohol's effects on the teenage brain helps them make the dangerous decision to drive drunk. In *Teens Under the Influence*, Katherine Ketcham and Nicholas A. Pace write that although alcohol does not sedate teenagers as strongly as it does adults, it has a more powerful effect on their sense of judgment: "While adolescents may be able to stay awake and keep drinking long after adult drinkers have tumbled into bed, their decision-making skills, judgment, and memory are more profoundly affected by the drug. They will think they can do things that they cannot do safely under the influence of [alcohol], and they may make decisions that put their lives or the lives of others at risk."[68]

On June 17, 2011, when eighteen-year-old Keaton Leon Hannah killed a father and his infant son when he drove his car head-on into their vehicle while driving the wrong way on a state highway, Hannah admitted he had been drinking but told police he thought he was still able to drive safely. Joseph, an online commentator reacting to a news story about the accident, criticized Hannah for making the deadly decision to drive after he had been drinking. Joseph wrote: "We have a situation where two people died because of someone's selfish decision to drive while intoxicated. Regardless of whether Hannah is a 'good' or 'bad' person isn't the issue here. The real issue is drunk driving [and] how much damage it does to families."[69]

A LIFETIME OF GUILT

"It has been very hard to deal with the guilt I feel because I love all three of them. I miss them so much and I think about them every single day."—Seventeen-year-old Bret Johnson after causing the deaths of three fellow Holt (Michigan) High School students while driving drunk on January 30, 2011

Quoted in Kevin Grasha. "Holt Teen Gets 4–15 Years in Prison in Fatal Drunk Driving Accident." *Lansing (MI) State Journal*, June 8, 2011. www.lansingstatejournal.com/article/20110608/NEWS01/106080341/Holt-teen-gets-4-15-years-prison-fatal-drunk-driving-accident?odyssey=nav%7Chead.

The unique psychology of teenagers can also lead them to decide to drive after they have been drinking. Sergeant Tim Bieber of the Clark County Sheriff's Office in the state of Washington has investigated numerous auto accidents involving alcohol. After several 2006 crashes involving intoxicated teenagers, Bieber said

Fleeing from Police

When drunk teenagers become involved with the police, their first impulse may be to run away so they will not be arrested. Hawk was sixteen when he passed out while driving and crashed his car in West Allis, Wisconsin. When police officers pursued him, he managed to elude them by running through a golf course. Hawk explains:

BAM, CRUNCH, BAM! I had passed out and my car veered across the right lane and the parking lane. I had gone up on a driveway and sheared off an aluminum light pole. [When I] restarted the car the belts were squealing. I drove half a block and turned right and parked. I knew the car wouldn't make it home. I started running and cut through a golf course when I heard sirens. I was on the railroad tracks when I saw the spotlights. I ran another ten yards and hid in the bushes. When the cops left, I continued on to my [dad's house]. When I woke up the next day he took me in to the cop shop [police station] to face the music.

Hawk had no choice but to turn himself in because police knew the car they found was his.

Hawk. Interview with the author, June 14, 2007.

When teens have been drinking and become involved with the police they often try to escape.

he believed so many teenagers risk driving after they have been drinking because of their naive belief that they will never be hurt or cause a serious accident: "A lot of it is this sense of invincibility [teens have]. Most kids that age don't think anything bad is going to happen."[70] That same feeling of invulnerability leads teenagers to ignore the need to fasten their seat belts. A 2008 study showed that 63 percent of young drivers involved in fatal crashes who had been drinking had not fastened their seat belts; in addition, 73 percent of drinking drivers killed in those crashes were not wearing seat belts. Some of those teens would probably have lived if they had worn seat belts, because the safety devices help reduce the severity of injuries in such crashes.

Drunk Driving

The reason the decision to drive after they have been drinking is so destructive for teens or adults is that alcohol severely decreases their physical and mental ability to drive safely. People who are drunk have trouble talking, walking, speaking, and thinking because alcohol makes it difficult for their brains to direct their bodies to perform even simple tasks like walking in a straight line. The effect alcohol has on the way people drive is similar but even more dangerous. Instead of piloting only their body, a drunk driver is also controlling a hunk of metal weighing several thousand pounds that can travel at speeds 100 miles per hour (161kph) or even faster. Cars driven by drunk drivers become mobile missiles that can injure or kill the driver, passengers, or other people if they lose control and crash or collide with a tree, bridge abutment, or another car.

Alcohol affects drivers in many ways: sight (vision becomes blurred and the driver has trouble seeing the road and other vehicles); motor skills (the ability to guide the car in a straight line, control speed, change lanes, or properly apply brakes); and the driver's mind (a weakened ability to understand what is happening to the car and to respond rapidly to changing road conditions such as oncoming vehicles or a traffic light turning red). The effects alcohol has on a person's ability to drive are related to the level of the driver's blood alcohol concentration (BAC)—the higher the BAC the more trouble drinkers will have driving.

One way to help teenagers understand how difficult and dangerous it is to drive when they are intoxicated is to create conditions that simulate drunk driving. On March 4, 2011, Chattahoochee High School in Johns Creek, Georgia, devoted a day to driver-safety lessons for its 1,730 students. One educational activity was to have students drive a car twice through a series of orange cones while wearing electronic goggles that simulate the vision of a drunk driver. During the first attempt the goggles simulated a BAC of 0.08 percent, the legal limit for drunk driving in all 50 states, and the second time the goggles imitated vision with a much higher BAC. Eighteen-year-old senior Catie Foley said the goggles made it hard to drive: "I knocked down a lot of cones at the legal limit. Then I put the totally drunk goggles on, and it was even worse."[71]

A similar lesson was conducted in May 2011 at Pottsgrove High School in Lower Pottsgrove, Pennsylvania. Students also drove a car twice over a course. During the second drive, a change in the steering column delayed their responses to turning the vehicle by

The Pain Lasts a Lifetime

Gary was a twenty-year-old college student in Milwaukee. He and his best friend were drunk and driving to a dance when Gary made a turn and drove into an oncoming taxi. The taxi smashed into the passenger side of his car, and his friend suffered six broken ribs, two broken legs, and a fractured skull. "They didn't think he was going to live," Gary said. When Gary finally saw his friend in the hospital, he told Gary, "If I ever make it out of here alive I'm going to kill you." Gary told him, "I don't blame you." The friend survived, but his injuries never fully healed; he has trouble walking to this day. More than four decades later, the broken friendship and pain of what happened to his best friend because he drove drunk still haunt Gary. He says: "It's still awful. It doesn't matter [how long ago it was]. For the last forty years I have held the guilt of this because I have accepted 100 percent of the responsibility of that, for nearly killing my best friend and crippling him. It has not been a good thing to live with."

Gary. Interview with the author, June 20, 2011.

seven-tenths of a second, the same time delay the brain would experience in making decisions to turn the car after the driver had drunk one beer. Liana Carvalho said she "ran over the whole line" of cones the second time, and Sarah Lockhead said she had so much trouble driving that she decided "it's not smart to get into a car with someone who has even had just a drink or two."[72] Students also attended an assembly in which parents of three students who had died in drunk driving accidents discussed how devastating the deaths had been for them.

Although teenage drinking and driving can have disastrous consequences, many teens do so without suffering any serious consequences. Mike drove drunk many times when he was a teenager. He was never arrested for drunk driving and never had an accident, but he did back into a car once in a parking lot; he fled before anyone saw him because he was afraid of being arrested. Even though Mike never got into trouble, he admits that driving drunk sometimes scared him:

> It sometimes seemed like fun, it was kinda goofy. But it's hard to see, sometimes it looks like there are two or three cars coming at you when there's just one. I liked driving fast when I drank. Sometimes curves seemed to just be there when I thought the road was straight . . . that was bad. I even ran off [the road] a few times. And I was always worried about the cops. I don't know why they never caught me.[73]

Despite the obvious effects alcohol has on people, tens of thousands of teenagers and adults decide to drink and drive every day. The results can be disastrous.

"I Would Do Anything"

One of the effects alcohol has on people is to make them feel brave enough to do dangerous things. Jack was known for accepting nearly any challenge when he had been drinking. He was driving through a park once when a buddy riding with him dared Jack to drive off the road for a joyride on the grass. Jack explains what happened: "I was driving in the car on the parkway. And one of the guys said, 'I dare you to jump the curb and drive down the hill by the creek.' So I did. But the hill was a steep one and the guys got frightened when I drove down it, they were screaming. I would do anything when I was drinking, I just didn't care what happened."[74]

In addition to making people brave enough to do dangerous things, alcohol robs them of the intelligence needed to make smart decisions about how they should be driving. Drunk drivers often drive too fast for conditions or try to pass other cars when they should not. On June 17, 2011, eighteen-year-old Cameron J. Mikutis of Monona, Wisconsin, was charged with homicide by intoxicated use of a motor vehicle and drunk driving. Mikutis told police he was being "(expletive) stupid"[75] on May 29 when he was driving his 1998 Chevrolet Malibu about 60 miles per hour (97kph) on a street in Madison, Wisconsin, a speed that was well above the posted limit. Mikutis lost control of the car, hit a parked pickup truck, and crashed into a tree. Seventeen-year-old Toree Gutzmer of Madison died June 7 of head injuries suffered in the crash, and a second passenger was severely injured.

UNHEEDED WARNING

"Two nights before his death, I reminded my son not to drink, and not to get into a car with anyone who had been drinking." [His son responded,] "Trust me dad. I know better."—Jeff Levy, discussing the death of his son in 2009 when the college student was a passenger in a car driven by a drunk teenager that crashed

Quoted in Susan Larson. "Parents, Teens Discuss Perils of College Drinking Culture." *Burke (VA) Patch*, July 26, 2011. http://burke.patch.com/articles/parents-teens-discuss-perils-of-college-drinking-culture.

Many teenagers often ride with friends because they do not have their own cars. Even if those passengers do not drink, they can be killed or seriously injured if they get into a car driven by someone who is intoxicated. On February 25, 2006, Jessica Rasdall and Laura Gorman, her best friend, went dancing at some clubs in Ybor City, Florida. Even though they were only eighteen

A Vermont state trooper checks the wrecked car in which four teenagers were killed. Many teens will take a ride with a drunk teen simply because he or she has a car.

years old, they were served drinks and got drunk. Gorman died when Rasdall ran off Interstate 275 and smashed into a tree while driving her friend home after the bars closed at 3:00 A.M.

Rasdall was sentenced to four years in prison after she pleaded no contest to a charge of driving-under-the-influence manslaughter. But Rasdall claims she will continue to serve a lifetime sentence because of the emotional pain she will always feel over the death of Gorman: "I killed my best friend. I never blamed it on anybody else. I had a big court hearing. I got up and I said, 'I drank, I drove and I killed my best friend.'"[76] The memories of killing someone were equally painful for Reggie Stephey. On June 24, 2008, Stephey was released from prison in Huntsville, Texas, after serving a seven-year sentence on two counts of intoxication manslaughter for killing two high school foreign exchange students while driving drunk in Travis County.

Stephey was eighteen when his truck ran into a car and killed Natalia Chpytchak-Bennett of Russia and Laura Guerrero of

Colombia. Three other exchange students survived the crash, but Jacqueline Saburido of Venezuela was so severely burned that all her fingers were amputated and her face was horribly disfigured. Stephey said the memory of what he did will always haunt him: "It's not something that I am going to forget. I did seven years [in prison but it is] a life sentence. It's [the memory of killing two people] something that's going to be with me every morning when I wake up and every night when I go to sleep. It's nothing I am going to forget about, nor would I want to forget."[77]

A Mother's Plea

Rosie Nevinger wants teenagers to understand how terrible it is when young people die in drunk driving accidents. Her concern, however, was with the daughter she lost in one such accident. On November 22, 2010, one hundred people attended a candlelight vigil at Santa Teresa High School in San Jose, California, for Jordan

A young woman leaves a courthouse after being sentenced to five years for a drinking-and-driving accident that killed three teens. The guilt and consequences of driving drunk can last a lifetime.

Mourners attend a "mock" funeral to show what it would be like if a classmate was killed in a drunk driving accident. Teens are urged to call their parents, friends, or anyone who can give them a ride home instead of getting in a car with a drunk driver.

Michelle West, a popular cheerleader who had died in a drunk driving crash several days earlier. West was one of four teenagers who were passengers in a car driven by a 17-year-old female student that crashed near San Jose. The teens had been drinking at a party, and open bottles of brandy and vodka were found in the wreckage of the Toyota RAV4. At the vigil, Nevinger delivered an emotional plea to young people to remember that drinking and driving had caused her daughter's death:

> I can tell right now, I smell alcohol and I know none of you are over 21 years old. And I know half of you are going to be getting into a car and driving. Do not let Jordan Michelle West's name go in vain. Do not. Call your best friend's mom. Call your godparents. Call somebody. Anybody will pick you up. You don't have to die. My daughter's dead.[78]

PREVENTING TEENAGE DRINKING

On August 2, 2011, in Topeka, Kansas, local government and law enforcement officials as well as representatives of private organizations held a Remembering Last Night initiative to curb teenage drinking. The effort was aimed at making teens aware of the "Remembering Last Night" Facebook page created by Hannah Helmke and Elijah Kampsen, eighteen-year-old recent graduates of Shawnee Heights [Kansas] High School. Kampsen said Facebook is a great way to reach teens with messages about dangers associated with drinking: "It's important to use social media to get in contact with youth."[79] The site allows teenagers to share information about drinking experiences and receive advice or help from other teens if drinking becomes a problem.

Topeka police chief Ron Miller said, "The emphasis [of such programs] has to be on prevention. It takes the entire community to prevent underage drinking. The community has got to get serious about preventing underage drinking."[80] Miller's comment echoed the African proverb "It takes a village to raise a child." In 1996, when Hillary Rodham Clinton was the nation's First Lady, she used that phrase for the title of her book *It Takes a Village: And Other Lessons Children Teach Us*. In the book, Clinton argued that everyone in a community should become involved in educating children.

The effort to curb teenage drinking and safeguard young people against the dangers of using alcohol also requires the effort of everyone in the community. That fight against underage drinking is being waged across the nation by government agencies, private groups, and even teens themselves.

Government Programs

Since underage drinking is both a legal and a public health issue, it is a concern for federal, state, and local government agencies. There are many federal government programs aimed at stopping teenage drinking. The scope of these programs is evident at Stop Underage Drinking (www.stopalcoholabuse .gov), the federal government's Internet gateway to information on underage drinking. The site has information about and links to programs that fifteen different federal agencies operate to combat teen drinking; even the Department of Defense fights underage drinking because alcohol can become a problem for

The Students Against Destructive Decisions (SADD) stages a scene of mourners and a coffin with a mirror in it to make a dramatic point about the consequences of driving while intoxicated.

young soldiers. State and local government agencies, especially school districts, are also working hard to curb teenage drinking. In Nebraska, Governor Dave Heineman declared April 21, 2011, the state's first annual PowerTalk 21 Day. Heineman encouraged parents to talk to their children about the problems associated with underage drinking because "what we say and do makes a big difference to our children."[81]

In addition to government programs, private organizations like Mothers Against Drunk Driving (MADD) and Students Against Destructive Decisions (SADD) fight underage drinking. Most of their efforts are aimed at educating teenagers and the general public about the many effects alcohol has on teenagers. Government agencies, individuals, and groups involved in this fight use a wide variety of methods to accomplish that goal.

Underage Drinking Education

It is easier than ever today to learn about underage drinking. A wealth of information is available on the subject in every medium possible, from books and pamphlets to videos and Internet sites. The Internet is one of the best sources about teenage drinking because it allows easy access to information from around the world. Sites have medical facts on the effects alcohol has on teens and ways parents can help teens cope with alcohol-related problems. There are also sites in which teenagers can discuss alcohol use with other teens or read what others have written about their experiences with alcohol. Schools teach students about the dangers of alcohol in classes and hold assemblies on the subject. Schools also try to give parents tips on how to talk to their children about alcohol and deal with them if they start drinking. In addition to such ordinary educational activities, many efforts to educate teens use creative means to help them understand the realities and dangers of underage drinking.

High school prom night is one of the most dangerous of the year for teenagers, who often combine drinking with the big social event. On March 25, 2011, the day before the prom at Alexandria High School in Anniston, Alabama, Calhoun County deputies staged a mock fatal accident at the school, complete with a smashed-up auto, empty beer cans, and two victims who were taken away by ambulance. The event was organized by the school's SADD affiliate to show students what can happen if they drink and drive. Sophomore Carly Edwards said the dramatization was an eye-opener for her: "It's scary. I'm sure this will send a message to some people who don't think about the consequences."[82]

IT CAN HAPPEN TO ANYONE

"People think, 'It's not going to happen to me' or 'I'll never drink that much again.' They do not seem to associate their own heavy drinking with negative consequences."—Kevin King, coauthor of a study on why some college students continue to drink despite problems associated with their alcohol use

Quoted in Molly McElroy. "Rose-Colored Beer Goggles: Social Benefits of Heavy Drinking Outweigh Harms." *UW Today*, July 5, 2011. www.washington.edu/news/articles/rose-colored-beer-goggles-social-benefits-of-heavy-drinking-outweigh-harms.

Imbler High School senior Kiley Dewey won a statewide award in Oregon for fighting drunk driving for the one-day Living Dead program she organized at her school on October 20, 2008. In the United States a teenager dies on average every fifteen minutes in a drunk driving accident. Over a three-hour period, Imbler High School students who were chosen to become those victims donned white makeup and hooded cloaks. When they went to classes in costume, they reminded other students about how many teens die in such accidents.

For many young people, drinking either starts or escalates when they go to college. When drinking at off-campus housing at the University of Wisconsin–Platteville became a problem because of loud parties and vandalism by drunken students, the SAFE (Safe Actions for Everyone) Grant County Coalition decided to act. In 2010 it started the Fresh Start program, which educated students about their out-of-control behavior instead of punishing them. Fresh Start allowed students to avoid being ticketed or fined for underage drinking by taking a course that taught them about the dangers associated with underage drinking. Kathy A. Marty, the group's director, said, "We want

One SADD alcohol-prevention technique has been to use virtual reality to simulate the effects of alcohol during a mock sobriety test.

to educate, too, not just penalize."[83] The group encouraged students to host nonalcoholic parties by awarding a cash prize to the best party each year.

In East Hartford, Connecticut, ERASE (East of the River Action for Substance Abuse Elimination) attacks problems like teen drinking by teaching young people how to develop media campaigns to fight them. Students also study existing policies in schools and their community about such subjects. Executive

Director Bonnie W. Smith said it is important that teens are involved in such programs because "evidence shows that a peer-to-peer message is far more powerful than someone speaking at someone else. When young people send the message not to drink, it's very powerful."[84]

"I SHOULD BE DEAD"

"I should be dead but by the Grace of God I am alive to pray that my kids won't be as stupid as we were [when he and his friends were young]."—Jacked Up Jerry in an online comment on June 7, 2011, to a newspaper story about the dangers teenagers face when they drink and drive

Quoted in Kim Painter. "Summertime Can Be a Breaking Point for Teen Safety." *USA Today*, June 17, 2011. http://yourlife.usatoday.com/parenting-family/teen-ya/story/2011/06/Summertime-can-be-a-breaking-point-for-teen-safety/48115904/1.

Although general education and innovative programs have helped curb teenage drinking, they have failed to stop it entirely. Teens that do drink, however, as well as adults who provide them with alcohol, risk being arrested and put in jail because of strict enforcement of underage drinking laws.

Teen Drinking Is Illegal

Few teenagers who drink ever stop to think that they could be arrested for doing so. However, it happens every day to hundreds of teens. On July 29, 2011, police in South Kingstown, Rhode Island, arrested two nineteen-year-old men who were camping out because they had more than one hundred dollars' worth of alcoholic beverages and small amounts of marijuana in their tent. The arrest came in a wooded area off a bike path, a spot so secluded the teens had thought they could drink there without being discovered by authorities. Police, however, were alerted by a woman who reported suspicious activity in the area.

Because it is illegal for teenagers to drink or buy alcohol, it is hard for them to obtain alcohol or go to places that serve it. Many teenagers get alcohol from older siblings or friends and

Parents Should Talk to Their Children

It is often hard for parents to discuss drinking with their children. Parents often have trouble because they do not know what to say about using alcohol, especially if they regularly consume alcoholic beverages themselves. However, psychologists and other experts on the subject of underage drinking stress that it is important for parents to establish a dialogue with their children on drinking even if they are worried about how to do it. There are many print and online resources that parents can use as a guide to the discussion. At the very least, parents should warn their children about the dangers of drinking. This is what author Emily Listfield recommends parents tell their children: "Ask your kids what kinds of experiences they're having; make your personal values clear, and calmly lay out the risks. Studies have found that parents who combine clear expectations of accountability with support and warmth have more success in curbing binge drinking than either strictly authoritarian or overly indulgent parents."

Emily Listfield. "Teen Drinking: What Parents Can Do." *Parade*, June 12, 2011. www.parade.com/health/2011/06/what-parents-can-do-drinking.html.

The National Center for Injury Prevention and Control operates a program that pledges parents to promote teenage driving safety and teach the pitfalls of alcohol on the highway.

some use fake identification cards. In Taunton, Massachusetts, illegal IDs became such a big problem during the summer of 2011 that police began a crackdown on them. Sergeant Kevin Medas admitted that new computer technology has made it easier for teens to fool bartenders or liquor store clerks with realistic fakes: "They have a way to duplicate it 90 percent."[85] Taunton won a $9,700 grant to increase its surveillance of underage drinking, including sting operations to find outlets that sell alcohol to teens using fake IDs. Medas warned that teens caught with liquor would be fined and arrested on misdemeanor charges of illegal possession.

Teenagers often have parties at home because police in many states are not allowed to enter a private home unless they have knowledge that a crime is being committed. In recent years, however, communities have begun passing laws to make it easier for police to arrest teens at such parties. On August 22, 2011, Bay Head, New Jersey, officials adopted an ordinance that allows police greater power to enter homes and break up underage parties. Bay Head mayor William W. Curtis explained why his city needed a stronger law to police teen drinking: "What concerns me the most is that it seems the drinkers are younger now. We used to get high school–age kids having the parties, but now we've had kids as young as 13 having drinking parties."[86]

The hosts of such parties, whether they are teenagers or adults, are committing crimes by providing alcohol to minors. On August 22, 2011, four teenagers were arrested at an overnight party in Merrimack, New Hampshire. Seventeen-year-old Danielle Belletate, who hosted the party, was charged with facilitating an underage drinking party as well as underage drinking.

Sometimes parents provide alcohol for teenagers at parties held in their homes. These parents claim it is safer to have their children and their friends drink in a controlled environment. But Brenda Nelson, a social worker in Barrington High School in Illinois, strongly disagrees with that argument: "I think that that is a myth that if they're drinking in my home then they're safe."[87]

Nelson worked to pass a social hosting law in Barrington that allows the city to fine parents who host underage drinking parties. Barrington was one of many Illinois communities that passed such laws after the 2006 deaths of two eighteen-year-olds. The teens were killed in a car crash after they had been drinking at a party in Deerfield, Illinois, that parents had held for their son and his friends. The deaths led many communities to pass laws to make it easier to prosecute adults who provide alcohol to minors.

ADULTS SERVING MINORS

"We're talking about kids who barely have their driver's licenses, and they're being served alcohol."—Saginaw, Michigan, police chief Gerald H. Cliff commenting on arrests at a bar that was serving teenagers

Quoted in Tom Gilchrist. "Police Ticket 15 Wednesday Night in Crackdown on Underage Drinking at Perry's Schuch Hotel." *Saginaw (MI) News*, August 18, 2011. www.mlive.com/news/saginaw/index.ssf/2011/08/police_ticket_15_wednesday_nig.html.

The belief that children are safer drinking at home was also proved false on July 27, 2011, when police in Las Cruces, New Mexico, arrested the father and stepmother of a fifteen-year-old boy who died of alcohol poisoning after drinking with them on July 14. They were charged with intentional child abuse resulting in death and negligent child abuse resulting in death. Police said the couple admitted allowing the boy to drink beer, wine, and brandy with them in their home. They even told police that while they were drinking together, the boy bragged about his drinking in text messages to friends.

One of the most effective ways in which states have fought teenage drinking is to lower the BAC level necessary to find teens guilty of drunk driving. The level of alcohol that is proof of intoxication for adults is 0.08 percent in all fifty states. Because teens are not allowed to drink, every state in the 1990s lowered that level for them to 0.02 percent or lower; some states have levels of 0.01 and a few 0.00, which is true zero tolerance. In 2005 Jeanne Mejeur of the National Conference of State Legislatures wrote that the laws were a factor in a 6 percent decline nationwide from 1993 to 2003 in incidents involving teen drivers who had been drinking. However, Mejeur noted that "despite the improvement, far too many young drivers are still hitting the road after hitting the bottle. Reducing their access to alcohol is critical in saving lives."[88]

The harsh reality of teenage drinking is that some teenagers will drink despite the best efforts of government agencies, private groups, and individuals trying to make them realize how dangerous drinking can be for them. There are several factors that account for continued teenage drinking even though it is illegal and often unsafe.

In the 1990s every state lowered the legal blood alcohol concentration (BAC) for teenagers to at least .02, some to .00. The adult limit is .08.

Various Types of Impairment at Different BAC Levels

Blood Alcohol Concentration (BAC)*	Typical Effects	Predictable Effects on Driving
.02%	• Some loss of judgment • Relaxation • Slight body warmth • Altered mood	• Decline in visual functions (rapid tracking of a moving target) • Decline in ability to perform two tasks at the same time (divided attention)
.05%	• Exaggerated behavior • May have loss of small-muscle control (e.g., focusing his eyes) • Impaired judgment • Usually good feeling • Lowered alertness • Release of inhibition	• Reduced coordination • Reduced ability to track moving objects • Difficulty steering • Reduced response to emergency driving situations
.08%	• Muscle coordination becomes poor (e.g., balance, speech, vision, reaction times, and hearing) • Harder to detect danger • Judgment, self-control, reasoning, and memory are impaired	• Concentration • Short-term memory loss • Speed control • Reduced information processing capability (e.g., signal detection, visual search) • Impaired perception
.10%	• Clear deterioration of reaction time and control • Slurred speech, poor coordination, and slowed thinking	• Reduced ability to maintain lane position and brake appropriately
.15%	• Far less muscle control than normal • Vomiting may occur (unless this level is reached slowly or a person has developed a tolerance for alcohol) • Major loss of balance	• Substantial impairment in vehicle control, attention to driving task, and in necessary visual and auditory information processing

* Information in this table shows the BAC level at which the effect usually is first observed, and has been gathered from a variety of sources, including the National Highway Traffic Safety Administration, the National Institute on Alcohol Abuse and Alcoholism, the American Medical Association, the National Commission Against Drunk Driving, and WebMD.

Why Do Teens Still Drink?

The 1986 book *A Six-Pack and a Fake I.D.* by Susan and Daniel Cohen is a serious look at the many problems drinking creates for teenagers. In the book, the husband-and-wife writing team admitted honestly that they had been underage drinkers: "We both drank as teenagers, even though it was illegal to do so just as most other teenagers did then and do now. In school we were shown anti-drinking films [and] we laughed at them and ignored their message."[89]

Psychologists at the University of Washington released a study on the reasons college students continue to drink even after experiencing horrendous hangovers, fights, and sexual contact. Researchers concluded that these consequences were not dire enough to stop a teen from drinking.

Like the Cohens, many, if not most, teenagers laugh off warnings about drinking from parents, teachers, the news media, and even other young people. The fact that so many teens reject such advice and set aside factual evidence about the dangers drinking poses to them is frustrating to those who are trying to curb underage drinking. Like many adults, Verdigris police chief Barry Lamb wonders why, with so many examples of the dire consequences of drinking, so many teens fail to appreciate the dangers of drinking: "How often can you say it? How much can you preach it? How many doors do you have to knock on so that we don't have these preventable tragedies like this on our highways?"[90]

The main reason young people ignore warnings about alcohol is that most have not experienced any of the serious negative consequences of drinking, such as killing someone in an auto accident or becoming an alcoholic. Jeff drank heavily all through his teenage years but says, "I never got into any major trouble as a teen."[91] Jeff admits he was lucky. He was pulled over by police once when he was driving while drunk, but they did not arrest him.

LESSON NOT LEARNED

"We want to forgive and overlook youthful indiscretions. [But by] not punishing the kids earlier, it becomes more serious as an adult problem."—Clay Abbott of Texas District and County Attorneys Association explaining why Texas should be harder on teens who drink and drive

Quoted in Diane Jennings, Selwyn Crawford, and Darlean Spangenberger. "As Teens Drink and Drive, Texas Only Talks Tough." *Dallas Morning News*, January 2, 2011. www.dallas-news.com/news/crime/headlines/20110102-as-teens-drink-and-drive-texas-only-talks-tough-.ece.

On May 30, 2011, University of Washington (UW) psychologists released a study on why college students continue to drink even after they have experienced negative results such as hangovers, fights, and sexual contact they later realized was

A Young Alcoholic

People who start drinking when they are teenagers face a greater risk of becoming alcoholics. One of the most effective ways for alcoholics to quit drinking is to go to meetings of Alcoholics Anonymous (AA). Even though most AA members are adults, teenagers are welcome at meetings. Danna F. quit drinking and started attending AA when she was fourteen. Some meetings are solely for teenagers, but Danna felt welcomed by older alcoholics and enjoyed those meetings even more. In 2009, after nearly a decade of sobriety, Danna explained how much the older alcoholics helped her; female members even gave her rides to meetings be-cause she was not old enough to drive. Danna wrote:

> My age mattered less than the fact that I identified as an alco-holic. I had a ride home even when it was out of the way or late at night. The women from my home group threw me a sur-prise high school graduation party and pooled to buy me a wonderful gift. From my first meeting until now, I remain in awe of the genuineness and un-conditional love of AA members.

Danna F. "The Young One." *Grapevine*, July 2009, p. 53.

Alcoholics Anonymous has meetings for young alcoholics or for both young and old together. AA programs have been found repeatedly to be one of the most effective ways to quit drinking.

inappropriate or even dangerous. Their research included on-line responses from nearly five hundred students who discussed their drinking. Diane Logan, a UW clinical psychology graduate student, said the study showed that students who had only minor problems from drinking kept using alcohol because they believed the benefits outweighed the risk that something worse might happen. Logan writes, "Until high levels of negative consequences are experienced, participants aren't deterred by the ill effects of drinking."[92] The same pattern of ignoring negative consequences that come from drinking can also lead adults to continue drinking despite problems alcohol causes them, including drunk driving arrests.

Alcohol's ability to entice people to keep drinking despite negative experiences stems from the strong pleasurable effects it gives them. But even though alcohol's hold on many teenagers is strong enough to make them keep drinking despite run-ins with their parents, teachers, and law enforcement officials, the vast array of programs to curb underage drinking are having a positive effect. In June 2011 a survey by SADD and Liberty Mutual Insurance of 2,294 high school students across the nation showed that only 6 percent said they would drive on prom night if they had been drinking. That compared to a 2009 study in which 90 percent of teens indicated they or other teens would be more likely to drink and drive after a prom than any other time of the year. SADD spokesperson Stephen Wallace said: "Underage drinking is never acceptable; however, these findings suggest that when schools enforce zero-tolerance measures at official functions they can be an effective way to curb that dangerous behavior behind the wheel. On the flip side, however, the findings also suggest that when school enforcement is absent, drinking and driving is more prevalent."[93]

The encouraging results of the 2011 survey show that efforts to curb teenage drinking are easing the problem even though they will never be able to eliminate it.

EPILOGUE

SHOULD THE DRINKING AGE BE LOWERED?

It was the morning of a University of Florida football game against the University of Mississippi, and Max, a nineteen-year-old Florida freshman, had been drinking. Two hours before the game in Gainesville, Florida, Max was so drunk that he had trouble answering a *New York Times* reporter who was interviewing students about whether the drinking age should be lowered from twenty-one. Speaking slowly and slurring his words, the drunk student said: "Per-son-al-ly, I do agree the age should be lowered. It will cut down on binge drinking." Throwing an arm over another student, he continued. "But we take care of each other. We will not let anyone drink under the influence." Realizing his mistake, he added, "I mean drive under the influence. I'm sorry. I'm drunk already. It's been a long morning."[94]

It is not unusual for college students to drink heavily before a sporting event, not even in the morning. Drinking is an accepted part of college life, even though most students are not old enough to drink legally. Studies show that 8 out of 10 students drink and 4 out of 10 are binge drinkers, which means they have had at least five drinks in one session in the past two weeks. The ease with which older teenagers obtain alcohol, whether they are in college or not, renders the drinking age of 21 almost meaningless in terms of stopping them from drinking. That reality and the fact that people 18 and older are considered adults in other legal situations makes many people believe the drinking age should be 18 or 19. However, lowering the drinking age is still a hotly contested issue.

Students at the University of Kansas rally to support lowering the drinking age to eighteen. Proponents argue that if eighteen-year-olds can vote and enlist in the military they should be able to drink.

Lower Drinking Age Arguments

Some people who believe the drinking age should be lowered argue that 21 is an arbitrary age to allow people to consume alcohol. In the past, Americans were considered adults when they turned 21 because it was the age at which they could vote. But the voting age was lowered to 18 on July 1, 1971, when the nation adopted the Twenty-Sixth Amendment to the U.S. Constitution. Also, the drinking age is 18 in almost every other nation, including Australia, Canada, the People's Republic of China, Israel, Russia, and the United Kingdom. In Italy and Germany the drinking age is only 16.

Cynthia Garcia Coll, a professor of education at Brown University, grew up in Puerto Rico. The drinking age there is eighteen, and Coll said Puerto Ricans allowed teenagers to drink at family parties to teach them how to drink safely. She claims it is foolish to prohibit older teens from drinking and then, in an instant, allow them to consume as much alcohol as they want just because they turn twenty-one: "In this country, we go from saying "No, you can't do it,' and then all at once, we say 'Yes, you can' without really giving them any guidance. It's not like age twenty-one is a magic time when people become responsible drinkers."[95]

John McCardell is the founder of Choose Responsibility, a group that wants to lower the drinking age. McCardell, the former president of Middlebury College in Vermont, believes the higher age creates dangerous drinking patterns for young people aged 18 to 20: "It's bad social policy and bad law. Prohibition does not work. Those [under 21] who are choosing to drink are drinking much more recklessly, and it's gone behind closed doors and underground and off-campus."[96] The group, however, recommends that a lower drinking age would also be bad policy unless it was coupled with increased education about alcohol—teens would have to pass a course on drinking to gain that privilege—and strict regulation of teens who do drink.

ZERO TOLERANCE

"The problem is the first drink makes the second easier and so on. . . . Your kids may drink, but they should know what your expectation is; and your expectation should be 'no drinking until 21.'"—Jeff Levy, whose son died after a college drinking party

Quoted in Susan Larson. "Parents, Teens Discuss Perils of College Drinking Culture." *Burke (VA) Patch*, July 26, 2011. http://burke.patch.com/articles/parents-teens-discuss-perils-of-college-drinking-culture.

McCardell developed this view by witnessing binge drinking on college campuses. Because teens cannot drink legally, some say that they drink more heavily when they have the opportunity. The results of binge drinking can be disastrous and even fatal because of deaths from alcohol poisoning and drunk driving accidents. In

July 2008 McCardell organized the Amethyst Initiative, which derived its name from the violet-colored gemstone ancient Greeks believed could prevent intoxication.

The effort involved college presidents who signed a letter that claimed "twenty-one is not working" and that as a result "a culture of dangerous, clandestine 'binge-drinking'—often conducted off-campus—has developed." The statement also said that the higher age seemed foolish because "adults under 21 are deemed capable of voting, signing contracts, serving on juries and enlisting in the military, but are told they are not mature enough to have a beer."[97] By 2011 the heads of 136 universities, including Butler, Colgate, DePauw, Duke, Holy Cross, Ohio State, and Vermont Law School, had signed the statement.

It is fairly easy for teenage college students to obtain alcohol because they attend school with so many students who are twenty-one and can buy it for them. But the ease with which older teens obtain alcohol is not confined to college students. When Hawk was seventeen, he began working for a heating and sheet metal company. After work he had no problem being served when he went to bars with older workers. In fact, Hawk said he and his fellow workers sometimes began drinking before they left their jobsite: "The foreman had brought in a chest refrigerator and always had beer for us. We downed three beers and then punched out."[98]

The fact that the national drinking age of twenty-one is unable to stop older teens from drinking is the main reason most people believe it should be lowered. However, opponents of lowering the drinking age have their own strong arguments. And polls show that more people in the United States oppose a lower drinking than support it.

Fears About Teen Drinking

In October 2010 Angus Reid Public Opinion conducted an online survey that showed that 69 percent of Americans support the current drinking age, while only 27 percent want to lower it. The poll numbers show the continuing fears Americans have about teenage drinking. An article in the June 2010 edition of the *American Journal of Public Health* supported retaining the drinking age of twenty-one by citing new knowledge about the dangers of teenage drinking. The article's authors, Henry Wechsler and Toben F. Nelson, wrote:

> The weight of the scientific evidence, evaluated by many experts and government agencies, demonstrates that the minimum legal drinking age of 21 years is effective public policy for reducing underage drinking and preventing the negative consequences that can result from underage drinking. The evidence suggests that making alcohol more available by reducing the minimum legal drinking age to 18 years will lead to an increase in drinking and related [problems].[99]

Relatively recent discoveries have shown that teenagers who drink may damage their brains, which are still maturing, and face an increased chance of becoming addicted to alcohol. Teenage drinkers may also suffer impaired memory and greater difficulty in learning, damage that will affect them not only while they are in school but for the rest of their lives. However, the strongest argument against lowering the drinking age is the reason Congress increased it in 1984 to twenty-one by passing the National Minimum Drinking Age Act—the high number of drunk driving fatalities involving teenagers.

TWENTY-ONE IS NOT REALISTIC

"Our current prohibition directed against the consumption of alcohol by young people (who can marry, serve in the military, vote, enter into legal contracts, and shoulder adult responsibilities) is clearly not working. We need to abandon this failed and demeaning folly and replace it with a proven, realistic, and successful approach to reducing drinking problems."—Ruth Engs, Indiana University professor of applied health sciences, who has studied teenage drinking

Quoted in David J. Hanson. "The Drinking Age Should Be Lowered: Interview with Dr. Ruth Engs." Alcohol: Problems and Solutions. www2.potsdam.edu/hansondj/YouthIssues/1053520190.html.

In 2007 the National Highway Traffic Safety Administration (NHTSA) estimated that the 1984 law had saved the lives of nearly twenty-five thousand Americans by making it harder for teenagers to drink and drive. Ralph Hingson heads the National Institute on Alcohol Abuse and Alcoholism (NIAAA). He opposes a lower drinking age for that reason: "We already did the experiment of lowering the drinking age [to eighteen in the 1970s], and traffic crashes went up. I don't think it's a good idea to go back and repeat a policy that made things worse."[100] Hingson is also a former vice president of Mothers Against Drunk Driving (MADD), a powerful opponent of lowering the drinking age.

Despite strong opposition, there have been sporadic efforts since 1984 to lower the drinking age, including legislation introduced in a handful of states. None of the attempts has succeeded, but backers of a lower drinking age keep working toward that goal.

An Emotional Issue

Individuals and groups on both sides of the issue have logical arguments and, sometimes, even statistical evidence to back up their stands on the issue. However, underlying philosophical beliefs and emotions people have about alcohol in general also play an important role in determining attitudes on the controversial subject. Gail Gleason Milgram has studied alcohol use for decades at Rutgers University. She claims that any issue involving alcohol will always be controversial because of the deep, divided feelings Americans have about alcohol: "We have inconsistent attitudes and behaviors about drinking, which are more complex and controversial than we like to admit. Despite the general availability of alcohol, the problems associated with its use make us uncomfortable, and we often prefer to ignore them altogether. Alcohol strikes an emotional chord in many of us."[101]

Introduction: Teens + Alcohol = Trouble

1. Quoted in Ian Silver. "Baby Killed, Teen Charged in Drunk Driving Crash." FOX23.com, June 17, 2011. www.fox23.com/news/local/story/Man-Baby-Killed-Teen-Charged-In-Drunk-Driving/qy0RJY0tc0WVPoJex0AvNA.cspx.

2. Kenneth P. Moritsugu. *The Surgeon General's Call to Action to Prevent and Reduce Underage Drinking 2007*. Washington, DC: U.S. Department of Health and Human Services, 2007, p. 1.

3. National Highway Traffic Safety Administration. "Teen Drivers." www.nhtsa.gov/Teen-Drivers.

4. Quoted in Jessica Vander Velde. "UF Freshman from Tampa Found Dead by Friends in Madeira Beach Condo." *St. Petersburg (FL) Times*, March 15, 2011. www.tampabay.com/news/publicsafety/uf-freshman-from-tampa-found-dead-by-friends-in-madeira-beach-condo/1157270a.

5. Quoted in Katherine Ketcham and Nicholas A. Pace. *Teens Under the Influence: The Truth About Kids, Alcohol, and Other Drugs—How to Recognize the Problem and What to Do About It*. New York: Ballantine, 2003, p. 69.

6. Quoted in Kevin King. "Man and Child Killed in Alcohol-Related Crash Near Verdigris." KTUL.com, June 7, 2011. www.ktul.com/story/14927449/fatal-accident-reported-near-verdigris.

7. Quoted in Jarrel Wade. "18-Year-Old Held on Murder, DUI Complaints in Verdigris Wreck." *Tulsa (OK) World*, June 17, 2011. www.tulsaworld.com/specialprojects/news/crimewatch/article.aspx?subjectid=450&articleid=20110617_450_0_Anyear382332.

Chapter 1: Alcohol: A Socially Accepted Drug

8. Ketcham and Pace. *Teens Under the Influence*, p. 19.

9. Susan Cohen and Daniel Cohen. *A Six-Pack and a Fake I.D.: Teens Look at the Drinking Question*. New York: Evans, 1986, p. 129.

10. Gail Gleason Milgram and the Editors of Consumer Reports Books. *The Facts About Drinking: Coping with Alcohol Use, Abuse, and Alcoholism*. Mount Vernon, NY: Consumers Union of United States, 1990, p. 1.

11. Quoted in Wolfgang Schivelbusch. *Tastes of Paradise: A Social History of Spices, Stimulants, and Intoxicants*. New York: Pantheon, 1992, p. 22.

12. Quoted in David T. Courtwright. *Forces of Habit: Drugs and the Making of the Modern World*. Cambridge, MA: Harvard University Press, 2001, p. 72.

13. 1 Timothy 5:23 (New American Standard Bible).

14. Quoted in Sharon V. Salinger. *Taverns and Drinking in Early America*. Baltimore: Johns Hopkins University Press, 2002, p. 137.

15. W.J. Rorabaugh. *The Alcoholic Republic: An American Tradition*. New York: Oxford University Press, 1979, p. 35.

16. Thomas R. Pegram. *Battling Demon Rum: The Struggle for a Dry America, 1800–1933*. Chicago: Dee, 1998, p. 8.

17. Quoted in Salinger. *Taverns and Drinking in Early America*, p. 184.

18. Quoted in C. Furnas. *The Life and Times of the Late Demon Rum*. New York: Putnam's Sons, 1965, p. 35.

19. Judy. Interview with the author, June 28, 2011.

20. Quoted in Laurie Davies. "21 Turns 20." *Driven*, Spring 2004, p. 23.

21. Ronald Reagan. "Statement on the Presidential Commission on Drunk Driving." Ronald Reagan Presidential Library, April 5, 1983. www.reagan.utexas.edu/archives/speeches/1983/40583c.html

22. Quoted in Richard L. Madden. "Six Northeast Governors Ask Drinking Age of 21." *New York Times*, January 31, 1985, p. 3.

23. Quoted in Davies. "21 Turns 20," p. 23.

Chapter 2: Why Teens Drink and the Effects of Alcohol

24. Quoted in Anita Sing. "Daniel Radcliffe: Why I Don't Drink

Alcohol Any More." *Telegraph* (UK), July 6, 2011. www.telegraph
.co.uk/culture/harry-potter/8614366/Daniel-Radcliffe-why-
I-dont-drink-alcohol-any-more.html.

25. Cohen and Cohen. *A Six-Pack and a Fake I.D.*, p. 1.

26. Smokeseek. "A Teen Aged Alcoholic." Experience Project,
November 24, 2008. www.experienceproject.com/stories/
Am-A-Member-Of-Alcoholics-Anonymous/377009.

27. James B. Jacobs. *Drunk Driving: An American Dilemma.*
Chicago: University of Chicago Press, 1989, p. 3.

28. Quoted in John Kreiser. "Teen Drinking Takes Toll on
Brain." CBS, February 11, 2006. www.cbsnews.com/stories/
2006/07/05/eveningnews/main1778434.shtml.

29. Mike. Interview with the author, July 2, 2011.

30. Quoted in Leah Odze Epstein. "An Interview with Alexandra
Robbins, author of 'The Geeks Shall Inherit the Earth: Pop-
ularity, Quirk Theory, and Why Outsiders Thrive After High
School.'" *Drinking Diaries: From Celebration to Revelation*,
April 29, 2011. www.drinkingdiaries.com/2011/ 04/29/an-
interview-on-teen-drinking-with-alexandra-robbins-author-
of-the-geeks-shall-inherit-the-earth-popularity-quirk-theory-
and-why-outsiders-thrive-after-high-school.

31. Quoted in Reid K. Hester. "Why Do Teenagers Drink Alcohol?" *Selfhelp Magazine*, April 4, 2009. www.selfhelp mag-
azine.com/article/teen-alcoholism.

32. Quoted in David E. Gehlke. "Mother, Son Detail Perils of
Teen Drinking." *Pittsburgh Tribune Review*, October 12,
2006. www.pittsburghlive.com/x/pittsburghtrib/news/pitts
burgh/s_474187.html.

33. Hester. "Why Do Teenagers Drink Alcohol?"

34. Jeff. Interview with the author, July 7, 2011.

35. Quoted in Janet Firshein. "Wendy: Freedom to Drink, or
Freedom to Live?" Thirteen.org. www.thirteen.org/closeto
home/stories/html/wendy.html.

36. Quoted in Barbara Strauch. *The Primal Teen: What the New
Discoveries About the Teenage Brain Tell Us About Our Kids.*
New York: Doubleday, 2003, p. 85.

37. Quoted in Guest. "The Welch Sisters, Co-Authors of the
Memoir 'The Kids Are All Right,' Recall Their Best—and

Worst–Drinking Memories." *Drinking Diaries: From Celebra-tion to Revelation*, January 26, 2011. www.drinkingdiaries .com/2011/01/26/the-welch-sisters-co-authors-of-the-memoir-the-kids-are-all-right-recall-their-best-and-worst-drinking-memories.

38. James R. Milam and Katherine Ketcham. *Under the Influence: A Guide to the Myths and Realities of Alcoholism*. Seattle: Madrona, 1981, p. 16.

39. Cohen and Cohen. *A Six-Pack and a Fake I.D.*, p. 9.

40. Harry Milt. *Alcoholism, Its Causes and Cure: A New Handbook*. New York: Scribner's Sons, 1976, p. 10.

41. Quoted in Rhett Morgan. "Man Charged in 2 Deaths in Wreck Near Verdigris." *Tulsa (OK) World*, July 12, 2011. http://www .tulsaworld.com/news/article.aspx?subjectid=14&articleid= 20110712_14_0_CAEOEr232294.

Chapter 3: Dangers for Teen Drinkers

42. Quoted in Ketcham and Pace. *Teens Under the Influence*, p. 45.

43. Quoted in Strauch. *The Primal Teen*, p. 27.

44. Quoted in *Frontline*. "Interview: Deborah Yurgelun-Todd." www.pbs.org/wgbh/pages/frontline/shows/teenbrain/interviews/ todd.html.

45. Quoted in Strauch, *The Primal Teen*, pp. 88–89.

46. Jack. Interview with the author, August 5, 2011.

47. Jeff. Interview with the author, July 9, 2011.

48. Quoted in Leah Odze Epstein. "Interview with L*anne St*kes." *Drinking Diaries: From Celebration to Revelation*, May 18, 2011. www.drinkingdiaries.com/2011/05/18/interview-with-lanne-stkes.

49. Greg. Interview with the author, August 5, 2011.

50. Quoted in Vander Velde. "UF Freshman from Tampa Found Dead by Friends in Madeira Beach Condo."

51. National Institute on Alcohol Abuse and Alcoholism. "Col-lege Drinking Is a Culture." College Drinking—Changing the Culture. www.collegedrinkingprevention.gov/niaaacollege materials/taskforce/Intro_00.aspx.

52. Quoted in Ketcham and Pace. *Teens Under the Influence*, p. 39.

53. Quoted in Ronald E. Bogle. "Pills and Alcohol Form Prescrip-

tion for Disaster." *Durham (NC) Herald-Sun*, March 5, 2011. www.heraldsun.com/view/full_story/12183014/article-Pills-and-alcohol-form-prescription-for-disaster.

54. Quoted in Barbara Kantrowitz and Anne Underwood. "The Teen Drinking Dilemma." *Newsweek*, June 25, 2007, p. 36.

55. Quoted in Guest. "The Welch Sisters, Co-Authors of the Memoir 'The Kids Are All Right,' Recall Their Best—and Worst—Drinking Memories."

56. Quoted in Mary Pickels. "Rape Victim Tells Uniontown Assailant of Nightmares, Pain." *Greensburg (PA) Tribune-Review*, June 22, 2011, p. 1.

57. Quoted in Jeff Mosier. "Date Rape Warning Given to Arlington Teens: Link Between Drinking, Rape Stressed After Possible Assaults." *Dallas Morning News*, September 28, 2006, p. 1.

58. Quoted in Katy Butler. "The Grim Neurology of Teenage Drinking." *New York Times*, July 5, 2006. www.nytimes.com/2006/07/04/health/04teen.html.

59. Quoted in Ketcham and Pace. *Teens Under the Influence*, p. 175.

60. Quoted in Firshein. "Wendy."

61. Quoted in Kantrowitz and Underwood. "The Teen Drinking Dilemma," p. 36.

62. Quoted in Ketcham and Pace. *Teens Under the Influence*, p. 69.

Chapter 4: Drinking and Driving

63. Quoted in WTKR.com. "Teen Charged with DUI Has Been Arrested for Alcohol Before." June 16, 2011. www.wtkr.com/news/wtkr-virginia-beach-crash,0,5947828.story.

64. Quoted in Kim Painter. "Summertime Can Be a Breaking Point for Teen Safety." *USA Today*, June 6, 2011. http://yourlife.usatoday.com/parenting-family/teen-ya/story/2011/06/ Summertime-can-be-a-breaking-point-for-teen-safety/48115904/1.

65. Quoted in National Highway Traffic Safety Administration. "Teen Unsafe Driving Behaviors." August 5, 2004. www.nhtsa.gov/people/injury/newdriver/teenunsafedriving/index.html.

66. Quoted in Painter. "Summertime Can Be a Breaking Point for Teen Safety."

67. Quoted in Strauch. *The Primal Teen*, p. 179.

68. Ketcham and Pace. *Teens Under the Influence*, p. 45.

69. Quoted in Craig Day. "Claremore Teen Arrested After Suspected DUI Crash Kills Man, Baby." KOTV.com, June 17, 2011. www.newson6.com/story/14927478/two-killed-in-friday-morning-crash-on-66-in-verdigris.

70. Quoted in Kelly Adams. "Driving While a Male Teen." *Vancouver (WA) Columbian*, September 24, 2006, p. 1.

71. Quoted in Larry Copeland. "Driving-Safety Clinics Help Sober Up Teens." *USA Today*, March 4, 2011, p. A3.

72. Quoted in *Pottstown (PA) Mercury*. "Pottsgrove Students Get Drunk Driving Lesson; Simulation Is Part of Pottsgrove's Effort to Combat DUI." June 2, 2011. http://pottsmerc.com/articles/2011/06/02/news/doc4de854f4bb3bc127706208.txt?viewmode=fullstory.

73. Mike. Interview with the author, August 16, 2011.

74. Jack. Interview with the author, August 5, 2011.

75. Quoted in Sandy Cullen. "Monona Teen Charged with Homicide Following Alleged Drunken Crash." *Wisconsin State Journal*, June 18, 2011, p. 1.

76. Quoted in Alan B. Goldberg. "Drunken Driving Crash Shattered Teen's Life." *20/20*, ABC News, June 2, 2009. http://abcnews.go.com/2020/story?id=7726721&page=1.

77. Quoted Stephen Kreytak. "As Stephey Goes Home, Survivor Saburido Wishes Him Well." *Austin (TX) American Statesman*, June 25, 2008. www.statesman.com/specialreports/content/specialreports/jacqui/stephey.html.

78. Quoted in KTVU.com. "Family and Students Hold Tearful Vigil Remembering Teen." www.ktvu.com/news/25886891/detail.html.

Chapter 5: Preventing Teenage Drinking

79. Quoted in Angela Deines. "Officials Unveil Effort to Prevent Teen Drinking." *Topeka (KS) Capital-Journal*, August 1, 2011. http://cjonline.com/news/2011-08-01/officials-unveil-effort-prevent-teen-drinking.

80. Quoted in Deines. "Officials Unveil Effort to Prevent Teen Drinking."

81. Quoted in Steve Cain. "Governor Supports Initiative to Prevent Underage Drinking." *North Platte (NE) Bulletin*, April 2, 2011. www.northplattebulletin.com/index.asp?show=news &action=readStory&storyID=20696&pageID=24 Governor supports initiative to prevent underage drinking.

82. Quoted in Steele Cameron. "Dramatization at Alexandria High School Illustrates Dangers of Teen Drinking, Driving." *Anniston (AL) Star*, March 27, 2011, p. 1.

83. Quoted in SAMHSA News. "Grantee Highlights for the STOP Program." March/April 2010. www.samhsa.gov/samhsa newsletter/Volume_18_Number_2/Grantees.aspx.

84. Quoted in SAMHSA News. "Grantee Highlights for the STOP Program."

85. Quoted in Charles Winokoor. "CARDED: Taunton Cracks Down on Underage Drinking." *Taunton (MA) Gazette*, August 14, 2011. www.tauntongazette.com/features/x183773 9463/CARDED-Taunton-cracks-down-on-underage-drinking.

86. Quoted in Bonnie Delaney. "Underage Drinking: Towns Take a Stand." *Asbury Park (NJ) Press*, August 23, 2011. www.app.com/article/20110823/NJNEWS/308230016/Under age-drinking-Towns-take-a-stand.

87. Quoted in Craig Wall. "Schools Hold Parents, Teens Accountable for Underage Drinking." FOX Chicago News, August 22, 2011. www.myfoxchicago.com/dpp/news/metro/ schools-colleges-hold-parents-teens-accountable-underage-drinking-social-hosting-laws-20110811.

88. Jeanne Mejeur. "Young Drunk Drivers." *State Legislatures*, April 2005, p. 15.

89. Cohen and Cohen. *A Six-Pack and a Fake I.D.*, p. 9.

90. Quoted in Silver. "Baby Killed, Teen Charged in Drunk Driving Crash."

92. Quoted in Molly McElroy. "Rose-Colored Beer Goggles: Social Benefits of Heavy Drinking Outweigh Harms." *UW Today*, July 5, 2011. www.washington.edu/news/articles/ rose-colored-beer-goggles-social-benefits-of-heavy-drinking-outweigh-harms.

93. Quoted in Matthew Sturdevant. "New Survey Says Few Teens Drink and Drive on Prom Night." *Hartford (CT) Courant*, April

18, 2011. http://blogs.courant.com/connecticut_insurance/ 2011/04/new-survey-says-few-teens-drin.html.

Epilogue: Should the Drinking Age Be Lowered?

94. Quoted in Kevin Sack. "21." *New York Times*, November 2, 2008. http://query.nytimes.com/gst/fullpage.html?res=9F0 1E4DD1438F931A35752C1A96E9C8B63&scp=1&sq=&st =nyt.

95. Quoted in Kantrowitz and Underwood. "The Teen Drinking Dilemma," p. 36.

96. Quoted in *Parade*. "Should the Drinking Age Be Lowered?" www.parade.com/articles/editions/2007/edition_08-12-2007/ Teen_Drinking#.TfJDhXZQolkTeen Drinking.

97. Amethyst Initiative: Rethink the Drinking Age. "Statement." www.amethystinitiative.org/statement.

98. Hawk. Interview with the author, June 14, 2011.

99. Henry Wechsler and Toben F. Nelson. "Will Increasing Alcohol Availability by Lowering the Minimum Legal Drinking Age Decrease Drinking and Related Consequences Among Youths?" *American Journal of Public Health*, June 2010, p. 990.

100. Quoted in *Parade*. "Should the Drinking Age Be Lowered?"

101. Milgram and the Editors of Consumer Reports Books. *The Facts About Drinking*, p.1.

DISCUSSION QUESTIONS

Chapter 1: Alcohol: A Socially Accepted Drug

1. Why is alcohol legal and socially acceptable to consume even though it is dangerous?
2. People at one time believed it was good to drink a lot of alcohol. Did the benefits they gained from drinking outweigh the dangers they faced by drinking so much?
3. The United States failed to stop people from drinking when it passed Prohibition in 1919. Why did people keep drinking even though it was a crime?

Chapter 2: Why Teens Drink and the Effects of Alcohol

1. Why do teenagers drink? List some reasons they decide to start using alcohol.
2. What factors make it easy for teenagers to think they should be able to drink even though they are not old enough to drink legally?
3. How does alcohol work in the human body to make people feel happier?

Chapter 3: Dangers for Teen Drinkers

1. Does alcohol affect teenagers and adults the same way? If there are any differences, what are they?
2. Is drinking a lot of alcohol more dangerous for women than men?
3. Can teenagers become alcoholics? Is it harder for teenagers than adults to develop drinking problems?

Chapter 4: Drinking and Driving

1. How does alcohol make it difficult for someone who is intoxicated to drive?

2. In what ways does alcohol affect teenage drivers differently than it does adult drivers?

3. Would you feel safe getting into a car driven by a drunk driver?

Chapter 5: Preventing Teenage Drinking

1. Do schools do enough to educate teens about the dangers teens face when they drink?

2. Are penalties for teenagers who drink, whether they are for having alcohol at a school function or driving while drunk, too harsh? Explain your reasoning for the answer you gave.

3. Some teenagers are willing to discuss the mistakes they made when they were drinking. Do you think that is an effective way to educate teens about drinking? Why or why not?

Epilogue: Should the Drinking Age Be Lowered?

1. Why do some people want to lower the drinking age to eighteen?

2. Why do other people believe the drinking age should continue to be twenty-one?

3. Do you think the drinking age should be lowered to eighteen? Why or why not?

ORGANIZATIONS TO CONTACT

Al-Anon and Alateen
1600 Corporate Landing Pkwy.
Virginia Beach, VA 23454-5617
Phone: (757) 563-1600
E-mail: wso@al-anon.org
Website: www.al-anon.alateen.org

Al-Anon and Alateen are fellowship groups for the spouses, children, and other relatives and friends of alcoholics. Al-Anon and Alateen are 12-step programs that provide comfort, understanding, and encouragement to the relatives of the alcoholic and to the alcoholics themselves. Al-Anon and Alateen publish the *Forum*, a monthly magazine.

American Council on Alcoholism (ACA)
1000 E. Indian School Rd.
Phoenix, AZ 85014
Phone: (800) 527-5344
E-mail: info@aca-usa.org
Website: www.aca-usa.org

The ACA is an information and referral service for individuals who suffer from alcohol dependence, their families, treatment professionals, and others who are seeking a broad range of information on alcohol, alcohol dependence, alcohol abuse, and options for recovery.

National Clearinghouse for Alcohol and Drug Information (NCADI)
PO Box 2345
Rockville, MD 20847-2345
Phone: (800) 729-6686
Website: http://ncadi.samhsa.gov

The NCADI distributes publications of the U.S. Department of Health and Human Services, the National Institute on Drug Abuse, and other federal agencies concerned with alcohol and drug abuse. Brochure titles include *Tips for Teens: The Truth About Alcohol* and *Underage Drinking: Myths vs. Facts*.

Students Against Destructive Decisions (SADD)
SADD National
255 Main St.
Marlborough, MA 01732
Phone: (877) 723-3462
Website: www.sadd.org

Formerly known as Students Against Drunk Driving, this peer-to-peer education, prevention, and activism organization works to stop teens from drinking and doing other things that will harm them. The group has thousands of local chapters throughout the United States, most of which function as school clubs.

Books

Nathan Aaseng. *Teen Issues: Teens and Drunk Driving*. Lucent, San Diego, 2000. This book discusses what happens when teenagers drink and drive.

David Aretha. *On the Rocks: Teens and Alcohol*. New York: Franklin Watts, 2007. An informative guide on alcohol and teens who drink.

Katherine Ketcham and Nicholas A. Pace. *Teens Under the Influence: The Truth About Kids, Alcohol, and Other Drugs—How to Recognize the Problem and What to Do About It*. New York: Ballantine, 2003. This book includes many interviews with teenagers who have gotten into trouble by drinking.

Barbara Strauch. *The Primal Teen: What the New Discoveries About the Teenage Brain Tell Us About Our Kids*. New York: Doubleday, 2003. This book discusses new information about the development of the teenage brain, including the effects drinking has on teenagers.

Christine Van Tuyl, ed. *Issues That Concern You: Drunk Driving*. San Diego: Greenhaven, 2006. A collection of articles on various aspects of drunk driving that is a good primer on the subject.

Periodicals

Reid K. Hester. "Why Do Teenagers Drink Alcohol?" *Selfhelp Magazine*. www.selfhelpmagazine.com/article/teen-alcoholism.

Emily Listfield. "The Underage Drinking Epidemic." *Parade*, June 13, 2011. www.parade.com/health/2011/06/what-parents-can-do-drinking.html#.Tf9IonY8hJF.

Kim Painter. "Summertime Can Be a Breaking Point for Teen Safety." *USA Today*, June 6, 2011. http://yourlife.usatoday.com/parenting-family/teen-ya/story/2011/06/Summertime-can-be-a-breaking-point-for-teen-safety/48115904/1.

Websites

Alcohol (http://kidshealth.org/teen/drug_alcohol/alcohol/alcohol.html). This site has a thorough explanation of alcohol, its effects, and the risks of drinking for teens.

Alcohol Awareness Research Library (www.clcoholstats.com). This site provides statistics and information about drunk driving and underage drinking.

Century Council: Distillers Fighting Drunk Driving & Underage Drinking (www.centurycouncil.org/learn-the-facts/underage-drinking-stats). Funded by alcohol producers, this site has statistics and information on teenage drinking.

Cool Spot (www.thecoolspot.gov). This federal government site helps teenagers learn about alcohol and the dangers of drinking.

Drinking Diaries: From Celebration to Revelation (www.drinkingdiaries.com). In this blog, women, including teenagers, write about their drinking experiences and how alcohol affected their lives.

Every 15 Minutes (www.every15minutes.com). This site educates people about drunk and impaired driving and includes a memorial wall with pictures and tributes to victims of such accidents.

MedlinePlus: Underage Drinking (www.nlm.nih.gov/medlineplus/underagedrinking.html). This site by the National Library of Medicine and National Institutes of Health offers information on the medical effects, consequences, and prevention of underage drinking.

New Life In Recovery . . . from Alcoholism (www.new-life-in-recovery.com/teenagealcoholism.html). This site about teenage alcoholics provides sources of information about how young alcoholics can quit drinking.

Partnership at Drugfree.org (www.drugfree.org). This site has information about alcohol and drug abuse prevention, intervention, treatment, and recovery for teens and young adults.

Stop Underage Drinking (www.stopalcoholabuse.gov). This site is the federal government's gateway to information on underage drinking and on programs fifteen federal agencies operate to combat underage drinking.

INDEX

PICTURE CREDITS

ABOUT THE AUTHOR

Michael V. Uschan has written more than eighty books, including *Life of an American Soldier in Iraq*, for which he won the 2005 Council for Wisconsin Writers Juvenile Nonfiction Award. It was the second time he won the award. Uschan began his career as a writer and editor with United Press International, a wire service that provided stories to newspapers, radio, and television. Journalism is sometimes called "history in a hurry." Uschan considers writing history books a natural extension of the skills he developed in his many years as a journalist. He and his wife, Barbara, reside in the Milwaukee suburb of Franklin, Wisconsin.